# JUDSON PRESS
## PUBLISHERS SINCE 1824

Practical guidance for leading holy lives.
She tackles the common fears of rising moms.

# SCHOOL
## Is Where the
# HOME Is
### 180 Devotions for Parents

## Anita Mellott
### Foreword by Dr. Michael Farris

**JUDSON PRESS**
PUBLISHERS SINCE 1824
VALLEY FORGE, PA

School is Where the Home Is: 180 Devotions for Parents
© 2011 by Anita Mellott
All rights reserved.

The names of all people mentioned in these devotions, including the author's own spouse and children, have been changed to protect the privacy of those individuals.

Judson Press has made every effort to trace the ownership of all quotes. In the event of a question arising from the use of a quote, we regret any error made and will be pleased to make the necessary correction in future printings and editions of this book.

Unless otherwise indicated, Scripture quotations are taken from the HOLY BIBLE, NEW INTERNATIONAL VERSION®. NIV®. Copyright © 1973, 1978, 1984, 2010 by Biblica, Inc.™ Used by permission. All rights reserved worldwide.

Scripture quotations marked AMP are taken from the Amplified® Bible, Copyright © 1954, 1958, 1962, 1964, 1965, 1987 by The Lockman Foundation. Used by permission.

Scripture quotations marked MSG are taken from *THE MESSAGE*. Copyright © by Eugene H. Peterson 1993, 1994, 1995, 1996, 2000, 2001, 2002. Used by permission of NavPress Publishing Group.

Scripture quotations marked NASB are taken from the New American Standard Bible, © 1960, 1962, 1963, 1968, 1971, 1972, 1973, 1975, 1977, 1995 by The Lockman Foundation. Used by permission.

Scripture quotations marked NLT are taken from the *Holy Bible*, New Living Translation, copyright © 1996, 2004. Used by permission of Tyndale House Publishers, Inc. Wheaton, Illinois 60189. All rights reserved.

**Library of Congress Cataloging-in-Publication Data**

Mellott, Anita.
    School is where the home is : 180 devotions for parents / Anita Mellott. — 1st ed.
      p. cm.
    Includes bibliographical references.
    ISBN 978-0-8170-1696-8 (pbk. : alk. paper) 1. Parents—Prayers and devotions.
2. Home schooling—Prayers and devotions. I. Title.
    BV4845.M46   2011
    242'.645—dc22

Printed in the U.S.A.

First Edition, 2011.

# Foreword

Have you ever thought about the precise wording of the Great Commission? It says:

> "Therefore go and make disciples of all nations, baptizing them in the name of the Father and of the Son and of the Holy Spirit, and teaching them to obey everything I have commanded you. And surely I am with you always, to the very end of the age." (Matthew 28:19-20)

The command does not ask us to make random disciples within nations; rather we are to *disciple nations*. How is that done?

God gave us an example in Scripture. Abraham was expected to disciple Isaac. Isaac was supposed to disciple Jacob. Jacob, head of a large homeschooling family of 12 sons plus a number of daughters, was expected to disciple his children. The 12 sons were to disciple their families and the discipled families were to be faithful tribes, and ultimately produce a discipled nation.

The family is God's intended principal method for discipleship.

The importance of all of this becomes apparent when we consider the passage that contains the command that Jesus told us was the most important of all.

> Hear, O Israel: The Lord our God, the Lord is one. Love the Lord your God with all your heart and with all your soul and with all your strength. These commandments that I give you today are to be upon your hearts. Impress them on your children. Talk about them when you sit at home and when you walk along the road, when you lie down and when you get up. (Deuteronomy 6:4-8)

We are to love God. We are to teach our children to love God. And we are to do this teaching as we go through the course of everyday life.

Accordingly, the spiritual significance of successful homeschooling cannot possibly be overstated since it directly involves the fulfillment of both the Great Commission and the Great Commandment. We are teaching our children to love God with the ultimate goal of discipling a nation.

The enemy of our soul wants to do everything possible to dissuade and discourage you from homeschooling. There is only one solution for this—spiritual nurture and encouragement.

Anita Mellot's delightful devotional, *School Is Where the Home Is: 180 Devotions for Parents*, is aimed at exactly the right point—encouraging parents with truth, admonition, and the promises of God.

Like all good books of encouragement, Anita's draws out spiritual lessons from the everyday events that arise in the process of homeschooling. We all can identify with these stories. Accordingly, we can all benefit from the spiritual insights and encouragements she draws out of each episode.

The lessons are written with a light touch but are able to connect each of us with that which is truly profound.

I always am encouraged when I see a new resource that will truly help parents—and let's be honest, we really mean moms, who do the vast majority of homeschooling—stay in the field to complete the harvest.

Anita's devotionals will warm your heart and help you to help your children to love God.

Dr. Michael Farris
President, Homeschool Legal Defense Fund

# Acknowledgments

The idea for this book sparked four years ago. I grabbed minutes here and there, but for the most part, it remained an idea.

After my high-risk pregnancy and the birth of our second child, a whisper in my heart grew to a crescendo: "Write to encourage others." I took baby steps toward that. This book is testimony to God's amazing ability to fan a spark into a fire and make it reality in a way only he can.

*Writing is a solitary process*, I thought in my naïveté. I now know better. This book wouldn't have been written without the support of many.

Deep thanks go to my precious family—my tween and husband in particular—who allowed me to pull back the veil and write from my heart. Thanks for giving me up to my world of words over the summer and Christmas break. I know you didn't quite get how I could be in the same room yet be miles away. Jim, how can I thank you enough for being Superdad all those Saturdays and evenings when I sat glued to the computer? My sweet, sweet tween, I wouldn't trade a minute, even the not-so-good ones, of our homeschooling experience for anything. Without you, no book would exist and I would have a deep void in my life. My dear little toddler, if not for you, I wouldn't be learning how to make the most of brief windows of writing time, and I wouldn't have a daily reminder of the miracle of hope. Mummy, your help allowed me extra minutes in my world of ideas. All of you are the best cheerleading squad.

Seedwriters—Ane Mulligan, Julie Garmon, Barbara Davidson, Barb King, Patty Smith Hall, and Nora St. Laurent—you are the best. Every writer needs friends like you who are all too familiar with the exhilaration and angst that are this writing journey. Patti Lacy, your no-nonsense advice is invaluable. Thank you for speaking truth to me.

Families, homeschooling or not, who allowed me to share your stories, thank you.

Ann Beindorf, you rock! Your homeschooling eyes reviewing the entire manuscript were a blessing. Carol Barlow and Debby Archer, you took on a mammoth task with joy—double-checking every Bible reference and quote. Thank you for freeing me to work on the book.

My prayer warriors—Mummy, Dania Davern, Sharon Ball, Shiela Catanzarite, my discipleship group, and homeschool support group—thank you!

Amy Wallace, you came alongside this nervous newbie, steadying my feet along this writing path—for that I am thankful. Jeannie Fulbright, thank you for giving your time and advice so freely.

Huge thanks to Rebecca Irwin-Diehl at Judson Press for believing in the project and for challenging me to take my writing to the next level. And to Kim Shimer, marketing director extraordinaire, thank you so much for answering my many questions and for all that you're done to market the book.

To all who played a part in this writing endeavor—through praying for me, sharing your experiences, or offering a word when I most needed a boost—my heart overflows to you even though I may not have mentioned you by name.

God bless you all.

My precious Savior and Redeemer, "Who am I, Sovereign LORD ... that you have brought me this far?" (2 Samuel 7:18). I am nothing without you. Your grace and love overwhelm me. May your Spirit breathe life over each written word to refresh, encourage, and bring hope to all who browse through these pages.

# Introduction

*I'm not the only parent who has rough homeschooling moments!* I leaned forward in my chair as parents shared candidly with each other at a homeschool encouragement meeting. As we prayed for each other, I realized what had been missing in my four years of home-schooling—encouragement from others who shared the same journey. Till then, I had homeschooled in a small town in south-western Georgia, without the benefit of such meetings. When we relocated to Atlanta, a world of homeschooling opportunities opened up for us, including regular encouragement meetings. Those meetings, without fail, strengthen and comfort me.

As I daily live the joys and challenges of the homeschool life, and lead monthly encouragement meetings, one thing is clear: homeschool parents are not superheroes. We're ordinary people seeking to live out God's extraordinary call on our lives—to home-school our children and nurture their hearts. Encouragement is a vital ingredient of that wonderful, sometimes challenging journey.

*What would it be like to have a daily reminder from God's Word that he is with us as we homeschool? What would it be like to have a resource that offered practical and spiritual helps for the times I doubt and second-guess myself, or I wonder if I'm doing enough, or fear grips me when my child starts asking questions about faith?* Those questions, flitting through my mind over the years, birthed this book. The devotion-als cover every facet of the homeschool experience, including a good bit of parenting, since parenting is at the heart of home-schooling. Drawn from our family's homeschool experiences, and those of others, most of the devotionals are anecdotal, delving into a biblical principle, with a "digging deeper" thought-provoking section or a practical resource.

The devotionals are categorized into:

- **A Faith of Their Own:** Encourages parents to guide their children into intimacy with God, to help them develop a personal walk with Jesus.

- **And a Child Will Lead Them:** One of the amazing benefits of home-schooling is seeing life though the eyes of our children and learning from them.

- **Gifts We Give Our Children:** Encourages parents to focus on the intangible gifts that we can give our children, and to be intentional about discipling children and nurturing their hearts.

- **Homeschool Basics:** Practical help and encouragement for each homeschooling day: communicating in school, planning, organizing, making decisions about curriculum, dealing with challenges—mental blocks, frustration, and perfectionism, and encouraging our children's potential.

- **Homeschool Foundations:** Highlights the biblical fundamentals of what homeschooling is all about and why we homeschool.

- **Homeschool and Family:** Handling the impact of homeschooling on every aspect of family life, like time, relationships, and marriage, with encouragement and practical tips to keep a balance.

- **Homeschool and You:** The impact of homeschooling on the primary educator: setting boundaries, pride, the importance of community, lightening up, tough love, dealing with disapproval, and comparisons, and encouragement of the primary educator, mainly the mother, to take care of herself.

- **Spiritual Vitamins:** Spiritual refreshment for parents.

As you browse through these pages, may the Holy Spirit breathe into your heart hope, encouragement, and strength for your homeschool journey. Know that you are not alone—others face similar ups and downs, and the One who led you to home-school walks beside you, ready to pick you up when you stumble and steady your feet on his path, for he is Emmanuel—God with us.

Following are a few helpful links to homeschool resources:

Homeschool Legal Defense Association:
www.hslda.org

A to Z's Cool Homeschool Curriculum and Homeschool
Information: homeschooling.gomilpitas.com

Review of curricula:
www.homeschoolreviews.com;
cathyduffyreviews.com

Research studies about homeschooling:
www.nheri.org

Biblical resources on communication:
artofeloquence.com

A biblical perspective on home education:
whateverstateiam.com

Insights into the way God made boys and what he intends
them to be: www.raisingrealmen.com

Information about homeschooling and participating in a
network of homeschoolers:
www.firstclasshomeschool.org
www.thebusyhomeschoolmom.com

# Hope

"The old order of things has passed away. . . .
I am making everything new!" (Revelation 21:4-5)

Lisa, my eleven-year-old, drew a stick figure on the magnetic drawing board that her sister Katy had just unwrapped.

"Now something cool's going to happen. Watch!" She slid the bar down its side. Seven-month-old Katy went down on her knees and ran her fingers over the toy's surface. She picked it up and turned it over, trying to find the missing figure.

"See, you do this." Lisa grabbed a star-shaped magnet and showed her sister how to stamp on the magnetic board. Soon the toy's gleaming white surface was as dark as the night sky. Then together, hand over hand, they slid the bar. Katy squealed and clapped her hands as black gave way to bright white.

A similar toy—a "magic slate"—was my favorite when I was a child. I loved the fact that no matter what my mistakes were, I could start afresh.

That's exactly what a new school year signifies: a fresh start, new beginnings. In Revelation, Jesus declares that the old order of things has passed, and he ushers in newness of life. The biblical meaning of "new" conveys a sense of freshness—something that hasn't been used before or become worn out. I'm grabbing hold of that hope as I begin a new school year. My mistakes and the challenges of the past are erased when I come to Jesus in humble repentance. He breathes new life into our school. I'm taking a step toward a new beginning this year.

*Thank you, Lord, for new beginnings, for hope.*

**Digging deeper:** For what new beginnings are you thankful?

# The Source

I can do [everything] through him who
gives me strength. (Philippians 4:13)

Catalogs surrounded me as I sat on the floor of our family room. ABeka, Sonlight, *Five in a Row*. Which curriculum should I buy? Though I had taught graduate and undergraduate journalism courses, being responsible for my daughter Lisa's education overwhelmed me. What did I know about teaching a five-year-old?

Yet my husband, Jim, and I had prayed, explored schools, and weighed the pros and cons of homeschooling an only child. It took more than a year before we were certain of God's leading.

The more I thought about homeschooling, the more I lay awake at night. What if I messed up her foundational years?

"Lord, I have no idea how to homeschool. Please help me," became my daily prayer.

Weeks later at church a sentence grasped my heart: "God *always* empowers you for the task he gives you." It reminded me of Philippians 4:13.

On our first day of school, Lisa slid her tiny hand into mine as we bowed in prayer. I knew then that Jesus would walk with us on this journey.

On our last day of school that year, as Lisa read aloud from her little Bible, I blinked back tears. Successfully homeschooling her hadn't rested on my academic qualifications and abilities, but on Jesus, my source.

That evening Lisa gasped when Jim handed her a certificate for completing kindergarten. Eyes sparkling, she refused to let it go until we promised to frame it. That certificate still has a place of pride in our home.

Every year since then, we've made our last school day special. It's a celebration of the end of a school year. And it's a celebration of God manifesting his strength through my weakness.

**Digging deeper:** What reassurance does Philippians 4:13 offer you?

# "Never Give Up!"

You need to persevere so that when you have done
the will of God, you will receive what he has promised.
(Hebrews 10:36)

On the first day of our homeschooling adventure, five-year-old Lisa and I walked toward our schoolroom, hand in hand. When she noticed something on the desk, she pulled away and ran ahead.

"Mama, Daddy wrote us letters," she greeted me as I entered the room. Then she pushed her note into my hands. "What's it say, Mama?"

*What a good idea!*

I read it to her. As I ended with "never give up," she chuckled.

Since then, Jim's notes have been the highlight of every first school day. Without fail, the notes to Lisa end with "never give up."

None of us ever imagined how special those words would become in our lives.

On the days when Lisa gets frustrated with schoolwork or struggles in an area of character development, I gently ask, "What would Daddy say?" Sometimes she rolls her eyes. Other times she smiles and says, "Never give up."

On the not-so-easy homeschool days when I wonder what I'm doing and if it's worth it, I remember never to give up.

The year I felt God leading me to write again, rejection after rejection piled up. Every time I opened an envelope only to read, "We're sorry. . . ," doubts would cloud my mind. *Am I supposed to be doing this? Did God lead me to write?* But Lisa would come up to me, put her arms around me, and whisper, "Never give up, Mama."

The Hebrew root from which the word *perseverance* comes means to remain steadfast despite obstacles. Never give up. Those words have become our whisper of hope in challenging times.

**Digging deeper:** What is your family's whisper of hope?

# Gifts for Our Children

Jesus answered her, "If you knew the gift of God and who
it is that asks you for a drink, you would have asked him
and he would have given you living water." (John 4:10)

Eight-year-old Lisa stood by the Christmas tree, turning over a
small green and white canvas shoe in her hands.

"Mama, why did we get this?"

We read the tag together: "Through the generosity of your
friends, children in a developing country now have shoes."

"That was nice of our friends to do that, Mama. But it would've
been more fun if they'd sent us the money instead." I held back
my laughter as I explained what a privilege it is to bless those
in need.

*How easy it is to focus on the material. What's the focus of my life
and my homeschool?* I wondered later as I remembered Jesus'
words, "Life is more than food, and the body more than clothes"
(Luke 12:23).

In John 4:10 Jesus' comment, "If you knew the gift of God and
who it is that asks you for a drink," implies that the woman at the
well was missing out on something of far greater value.

As homeschooling parents we lay a strong academic foundation for our children. But there are gifts of greater value to offer:
introducing them to Jesus, who will never leave them nor forsake them, encouraging them in spiritual disciplines, and developing confidence in who they are in Christ. We mold their
character and their ability to see themselves as people created in
the image of God, provide a safe family atmosphere, and show
unconditional love—gifts worth so much more than the world
can ever give.

**Digging deeper:** What gifts are your focus?

*Wise hsing goals.*

# He Watches Over Me

He will not let your foot slip—he who watches
over you will not slumber. (Psalm 121:3)

Several four- to five-year-olds clustered around a LEGO table,
oblivious to the worship band on the screen in the family area of
our church. A little girl leaned forward to grab one of the trains.
She slipped and ended up under the table with the chair on top
of her. Her eyes grew wide. But before a cry escaped her lips, her
father covered the length of the room and swept her into his
arms. He held her in one arm while he righted the chair. Then he
swung her to him, looked her up and down, and smiled. Turning
her away from him, he sat her in the chair. Within seconds she
was engrossed with the LEGO toys. He drew up a chair a little
way behind her and sat there for the rest of the service.

I don't remember the sermon or the songs we sang that Sunday. But an image is still fresh in my mind—a father watching
over his daughter as he sat close enough to help if needed, far
enough not to hover.

It reminds me that I'm not alone in life or in my homeschool.
My Father is near—close enough to reach out and steady me
when I stumble or pick me up when I fall. He counsels me,
instructs me, and guides each step I take.

"The LORD will keep you from all harm—he will watch over
your life; the LORD will watch over your coming and going both
now and forevermore" (Psalm 121:7-9).

**Digging deeper:** What reassurance does Psalm 121 offer as you
homeschool?

Rcvg. const. criticism . . .

# Don't I Do Anything Right?

My children, listen when your father corrects you. Pay attention and learn good judgment. (Proverbs 4:1, NLT)

"You make some good points, Lisa, and you're a good writer." I looked up from her seven-paragraph essay. "But I don't think you should use such a conversational tone." I handed my twelve-year-old her corrected essay.

Her eyes pooled with tears. "You don't like it?"

I stared at her. "How did you get that idea?"

She pushed the paper around. "You don't like the conversational tone. Don't I do *anything* right?"

"Just because I don't think the tone is appropriate for a formal essay doesn't mean I don't like the essay. It's good."

Lisa stood and left the room.

I watched her as she trudged upstairs. *Lord, how do I encourage her to receive instruction graciously and realize it's not about her?*

The answer was long in coming.

On the last day of that semester, we read a chapter from Elizabeth George's *A Young Woman's Guide to Making Right Choices* during our devotions before school. Lisa was supposed to read a list of verses and discuss how they applied to her attitudes toward school.

She began to read Proverbs 4:1 (NLT): "My children, listen when your father corrects you. Pay attention and learn good judgment." Her voice faltered. After a few minutes, she looked at me. "I guess it means that I should listen to what you tell me in school—like with my essay."

I smiled. "Good judgment also helps you understand that correction isn't about you personally."

That morning I was encouraged. Scripture had planted seeds of awareness in her heart. I trusted that it would complete its transformative work in her heart.

**Digging deeper:** How do you give and receive instruction?

# Communicating in School

The Teacher sought to find just the right words
to express truths clearly. (Ecclesiastes 12:10, NLT)

I held up a new Latin flash card. Lisa laughed as she read out *"audācia."* "That's easy. I know the meaning."

"Why is it easy?"

"Don't you remember, Mom?" My twelve-year-old's eyes twinkled when I shook my head. "You were mad at me a few weeks ago and said, 'How can you have the audacity to talk to me like that?' And I asked, 'What does *audacity* mean?'" Her laughter pealed through the room.

I studied the deep patina of the dining table. *Lord,* I prayed, *help me not to respond in the heat of the moment.*

Since then I've found valuable communication advice in Scripture:

**Avoid quick responses.** The Teacher searched for "just the right words" (Ecclesiastes 12:10). That encouraged me to take time to think before I speak. It brought my grandmother's words to mind: "Count to three before responding, especially if you're annoyed."

**Watch the nonverbal.** My body language and paralanguage (tone of voice, volume) send powerful messages that either reinforce or refute my words. "Let us not love with words or speech but with actions and in truth" (1 John 3:18) is a reminder to let my actions speak louder than my words.

**Set boundaries.** "All you need to say is simply 'Yes' or 'No'" (Matthew 5:37). Clarity of instructions and expectations in school help avoid frustration that might lead to emotional responses.

*Excellent suggestions!*

**Practice gentleness.** "A gentle answer turns away wrath, but a harsh word stirs up anger" (Proverbs 15:1). Gentleness doesn't preclude being firm. Firm words spoken in gentleness and love go further than ones spoken in anger or frustration and have a greater impact on children.

**Digging deeper:** Make this your daily prayer: *Lord, let the words of my mouth, especially during school, be acceptable in your sight.*

[ Homeschool and You ] **DAY** 8

# Credibility

Then the chief cupbearer said to Pharaoh, "Today I am reminded of my shortcomings." (Genesis 41:9)

"Mom, want to play on the Wii with me?" Eleven-year-old Lisa waved her new Wii Sports Resort game in the air.

"Sure. Give me a few minutes." I continued breading the chicken.

After I put the pan in the oven, little Katy's cries sidetracked me. Time blurred as I attended to my mother, corrected school-work, and got dinner on the table on time.

As I chased Katy through the family room to keep her from climbing upstairs, I noticed the Wii menu on the TV screen. My heart pounded as I came to a halt. I turned to Lisa who was clearing the table. "I'm *so* sorry." My words came out in a rush. "I completely forgot I promised to play with you. I got distracted. Will you forgive me?" I hugged her.

Her arms still around me, she said, "Yes, Mom. I know you were busy." But when she looked at me, her eyes were dull.

"I'll make it up to you tomorrow. Next time please remind me about my promises." She slowly nodded then grinned.

The Bible is firm about the importance of keeping our word. According to Psalm 15, those who keep their word "even when it hurts" (v. 4, NLT) will dwell in God's sanctuary and ascend his

*' Saying 'it is the same as a promise !'*

holy hill. When we walk the talk, it goes a long way in building credibility.

I'm trying to be more aware of what I say I'll do and not to make promises when I'm busy. I want to be a person of integrity who can be relied on and who keeps promises even when it hurts.

**Digging deeper:** How do you build credibility with your children? Reflect on Genesis 40–41.

[ Homeschool and Family ] **DAY** 9

# Communicating and rudeness

Let your conversation be always full of grace,
seasoned with salt. (Colossians 4:6)

"Do you want this?" Jim held up a magazine as he sorted through the mail on the kitchen counter.

I nodded.

"Where should I put it?"

"Figure it out, Jim." I was trying to put a sippy cup in the already-full dishwasher and keep Katy from climbing onto its open door. In the background, Lisa kept up a minute-by-minute account of her day. My aging mother circled the kitchen trying to be helpful.

Jim's face reddened. "I was just trying to help," he muttered, his jaw tense.

Later that night, he informed me, "You were rude."

"*I* was rude? Couldn't you see I was in the middle of chaos?"

"You want me to share my feelings, and when I do you get upset."

It's hard to hear my faults—"How painful are honest words!" (Job 6:25). I want to defend myself, and some days I have good excuses. But change can come only with an open heart that is willing to learn: "Teach me, and I will be quiet; show me where I have been wrong" (Job 6:24).

**9**

Good communication is challenging even after sixteen years of marriage. In the midst of multitasking and trying to meet everyone's needs, it's hard to remember that communication is more than words. Effective communication takes time and effort—things I run short of on most days.

These days Jim knows not to expect much of me when I'm busy. I make an effort to stop what I'm doing to give him my attention. As we are more aware of what might lead to misunderstandings, we're better able to communicate with each other.

**Digging deeper:** What do you do to avoid misunderstandings? Reflect on Colossians 4:6.

# Speaking Life

When Jesus reached the spot, he looked up and said to him, "Zacchaeus, come down immediately. I must stay at your house today." So he came down at once and welcomed him gladly. (Luke 19:5-6)

"Mom." I looked up from checking Lisa's math problems. "I'm really nervous."

"About what?" I patted the chair next to me at the kitchen table.

"Well," my eleven-year-old began twisting her hands. "It's the testing . . . it's math."

For some reason, math was a challenge this year. *Forgive me, Lord, for not building up her confidence.*

"I'm—I'm math challenged!" she blurted, and shoved the chair away.

As I wondered what to say, I remembered Jesus speaking words of affirmation to Zacchaeus. Zacchaeus's position as chief tax collector didn't endear him to people; instead distrust followed him. Yet, Jesus singled him out of the crowds milling around to get a glimpse of the Rabbi. Looking straight at him, Jesus said, "Zacchaeus, I'm coming to your house today"—a show of faith in one who was despised. At Jesus' words, I can picture Zacchaeus slipping and sliding down that tree faster than my toddler on a giant-iced slide. Then Zacchaeus gave away half of what he owned to the poor and made restitution four times over. A life transformed.

I turned to face Lisa. "Sweetie, you'll be fine. I know you can do well. Pray and do your best."

She peered at me through her bangs. "You think I can do well?"

"I *know* you will."

She searched my eyes. Then she walked away, shoulders straighter, head held high. That's the affirming power of speaking life into someone.

**Digging deeper:** How can you affirm your children today? Reflect on Luke 19:1-10.

[ Homeschool Basics ] **DAY**  11

# Flexibility

And the peace of God, which transcends all understanding, will guard your hearts and your minds in Christ Jesus. (Philippians 4:7)

On our first day of middle school, I looked around our "classroom." A new computer at the kitchen desk, books and paper stacked on one end of the kitchen table, and schedules on the fridge. Excitement coursed through me—we were ready.

Reality hit after the first few days. Fifteen-month-old Katy wanted to join us at the kitchen table. She pulled books off the table faster than we could pick them up. She ignored the paper I gave her and scribbled on her sister's math work sheets instead. Her pounding on the table drowned out my voice. Play stations, rotating time between the girls—nothing seemed to work. By the end of the first month, I was frazzled and exhausted. Plans that had looked so good on paper remained on paper.

The churning within spilled over into irritability with my family, until Philippians 4:7 lodged itself in my heart. "Lord," I prayed, "please let your peace guard my heart and mind as we do school with a toddler around."

Change didn't come overnight. But by the end of the first semester, we did math with my toddler on my lap, scribbling on her sheets. Although Katy "read" aloud from her books while I taught Lisa, she didn't disturb me as much. Breaks throughout the day provided play time with Katy.

Change had come to our school, beginning with me. As I allowed God's peace to rule within, it overflowed into our home and school. With God's help, I'm still taking baby steps toward flexibility and learning to go with the flow.

**Digging deeper:** What stresses are you experiencing with school? Reflect on Isaiah 26:3-4.

[ Homeschool Basics ] **DAY** 12

# Back to the Drawing Board

Commit everything you do to the LORD. Trust him, and he will help you. (Psalm 37:5, NLT)

Within the first few weeks of middle school, I found myself back at the drawing board. My carefully planned schedules didn't hold up with a feisty little fifteen-month-old. Katy ignored the toys, books, and toddler-sized desk and chair. She wanted to be right where Lisa and I were. More than that, she wanted my attention focused on *her*.

*Plus, toddlers can learn what 'no!' means.*

"Rotate play stations." "Give her something she likes doing." "*Make* her stay on the blanket for a certain period of time." I sighed as I thought of the various suggestions my friends had made. None of them worked.

"Lord," I prayed, "why aren't any of these suggestions working? How am I going to teach Lisa?" We were already behind in school, and I was uptight.

Days later in my quiet time when I read Psalm 37:5, it became my prayer. "Lord, I'm committing everything I do to you and trusting you to help me find a way to do school with an eleven-year-old and a toddler."

I began to use windows of time that I hadn't been aware of before. When Katy awoke, I put aside my work for reading and snuggle time with her. That special time together early in the morning satisfied her. She wasn't so demanding when Lisa and I had devotions together and tackled math. While Lisa had self-directed study time, Katy and I colored or played with blocks.

Within a few weeks, we had caught up on school. I didn't have to get frazzled about my plans not working out. I just needed to go to the Master Planner for wisdom and peace.

**Digging deeper:** When have God's plans been better than yours?

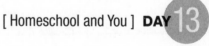

[ Homeschool and You ] **DAY** 13

# Appearances

The Lord said to Samuel, "The Lord does not look at the things people look at. People look at the outward appearance, but the Lord looks at the heart." (1 Samuel 16:7)

"Lisa, are you listening?"

Her head twisted around from the window. "Yes, Mama."

"Then look at the board." I turned and continued to draw and explain the parts of a cell.

As my eight-year-old's fingers tapped a rhythm on the desk, I glanced at her. "Pay attention." She was gazing out of the window again.

"That's it!" I walked over to the desk and stood in front of her. "What was I saying about cells?"

"Oh, sorry, Mama." She looked up at me and repeated my explanation word for word. I fumbled for the chair and sat down. After a few minutes, I broke the silence. "Good for you, sweetie." I reached across and patted her shoulder. "I didn't think you were listening. I'm sorry." She gave me a sheepish grin.

I was reminded that day not to judge by appearances. Often, my daughter's way of responding is different than mine. Instead of forming an opinion from my perspective, I need to see things from her point of view. I'd do well to keep that in mind in my interactions with others.

**Digging deeper:** When have appearances been deceptive in your homeschool? Reflect on 1 Samuel 16:1-13.

[ Homeschool Foundations ] **DAY** 14

# Purpose in the Calling

We constantly pray for you, that our God may count
you worthy of his calling. (2 Thessalonians 1:11)

"Sometimes it's nice to be in a co-op class you're not helping with, Mommy." Nine-year-old Lisa sat at the kitchen table working on history.

Each word pierced. "Well, if that's the way you feel, maybe you should be in school!" I stomped upstairs.

Deeply hurt, I ignored the knocks on my door and her cries of "That's not what I meant, Mommy. I like being at home and you teaching me."

As I thought about how much I had poured into her, I grabbed a towel to muffle my sobs. *What did she mean, Lord? How could she feel that way?*

*[handwritten marginal note, left side, rotated: "That was the response of a 10 yr. old. Plus, to mommy I say "Grow up!""]*

I threw the towel down and began vacuuming to work off my hurt and frustration.

As I cleaned, a gentle whisper filled my heart. *Why do you homeschool?*

I froze. "Because you called me to, Lord." Whether Lisa liked being homeschooled or not, or whether she appreciated me or not didn't matter. I *had* to obey a higher calling.

I went downstairs.

Lisa hunched over the table, her head in her hands. I touched her shoulder. My heart tightened when I saw her tear-streaked face.

"Mommy, I'm *so* sorry. I didn't mean to hurt you." Her words tumbled out.

"I'm the one who should apologize. Will you forgive me?" She took my hand as I reached for hers.

I explained why we homeschooled. She shared that she liked the sense of independence when I wasn't in the same classroom. I had misunderstood her.

Homeschooling isn't always easy. I stumble along the path sometimes, but God's calling on my life gives me purpose.

**Digging deeper:** How does 2 Thessalonians 1:11-12 steady you on your homeschooling path?

[ Homeschool and Family ] **DAY** 15

# Date Your Child!

For there will be a time for every activity, a time to judge every deed. (Ecclesiastes 3:17)

"Jim, what should I do?"

"What's going on?" He looked up from his book.

"Today wasn't a good school day." I touched the dark circle my tears had left on the sofa and rubbed the dampness deeper into the suede. "I don't want Lisa's memories of me being bad ones. I *want* to have good times with her."

He reached over and patted my hand. "It's going to be okay."

"That's what you always say." I glared at him.

He looked at me over his glasses and shrugged. "Well, then, date her!"

A smile spread across my face. That was it! We needed time together away from school—mommy-daughter time not student-teacher time.

The next day, as we walked out of Chuck E. Cheese's, a little hand slid into mine. "That was the best time ever, Mommy." I tightened my grip on her hand.

Our special times together have grown in value over the years, especially after my second child was born and adolescence hit.

Over the years, we've found:

- **"Dates" can be simple and inexpensive.** A walk, a manicure at home, or reading a favorite book together suffices. What's important is making the time to connect.
- **Consistency is important.** Our "dates" are a standing appointment on my calendar. My daughter knows they are a priority for me, and we look forward to our special one-on-one time.
- **Taking turns choosing what to do is a good idea.** We try to alternate each date with something that appeals to the other.

There's a time for everything—including time to strengthen parent-child relationships.

**Digging deeper:** Reflect on Ecclesiastes 3:1-8. Surprise your children with a special, fun date.

# The Block

With your help I can advance against a troop;
with my God I can scale a wall. (Psalm 18:29)

"I don't get it." Eleven year-old Lisa glared at her pre-algebra book.

"What don't you get?"

"This." She jabbed the book. I glanced at the open pages.

"Why?" I turned to her. "We've worked with decimals before."

She spun away from the desk. "I'm just dumb!" She ran upstairs to her room.

*Lord, help me.*

We had encountered mental blocks with math before, but this was the first time one had stuck around our school for several weeks.

*see pg. 14.*
*I guess she learned that from mom!*

How did we get it to slink away, tail between its legs?

Faith was the most important ingredient. Holding on to God's promises reassured us. As we worked our way through the block, Psalm 18, a magnificent portrait of God's power in rescuing David from the hand of Saul, infused me with hope. Verse 1, which declares, "I love you, LORD, my strength," reminded me of where our strength lay—in the Lord, not in my ability to explain concepts to Lisa or in her intelligence. God would give understanding.

When I wondered if we'd ever make it, verse 2 reminded me that "the LORD is my rock, my fortress and my deliverer." God would see us through the difficulties.

In our distress we called to the Lord for help (v. 6). When it was hard to see the end, God kept "my lamp burning" and turned Lisa's "darkness into light" (v. 28).

Because of the Lord, we had confidence that the huge wall that loomed in front of us would be scaled (v. 29). Jesus would bring us to a "spacious place" and rescue us (v. 19).

**Digging deeper:** How does faith help you during challenging school moments?

# Battling the Block— Part 1

I instruct you in the way of wisdom and lead you
along straight paths. (Proverbs 4:11)

Over the weeks as we continued to pray and battle the block, the
Lord's wisdom and guidance were evident. Here's what he
showed us to do:

**Recognize your differences.** Lisa and I are "fearfully and
wonderfully made" (Psalm 139:14). Both of us are unique, with
different approaches to problems. I keep at something until I get
it. She needs time and space. I prayed for discernment and
"depth of insight" (Philippians 1:9) in handling our differences.

**Step back.** After finding out the hard way that following my
approach only made a difficult situation worse, I found freedom
in stepping back. We took impromptu breaks for walks, games,
and music. We didn't even work on math for several days. It
helped us relax and connect during a stressful time so we could
return to math refocused and renewed.

**Try something else.** Flexibility is one of the blessings of homeschooling. We tried different approaches—computer games,
math games, online tutoring, a willing friend who explained the
concepts—to see what worked. We worked with different curricula—the spiral approach, the unit approach, manipulatives, a
computer-based program, DVD teaching—until we found the
right fit.

We even played around with our school schedule: When was
the best time to do math? Lisa suggested tackling math after she
finished English, since working on her favorite subject boosted
her confidence and self-esteem.

**Digging deeper:** Read "How to Survive a Learning Plateau,"
by Melanie Hexter, in *Homeschool Enrichment Magazine*,
July/August 2010.

*Good resource to check out.*

# Battling the Block— Part 2

Because the Sovereign LORD helps me, I will not be disgraced. Therefore have I set my face like flint, and I know I will not be put to shame. (Isaiah 50:7)

This verse paints an eloquent picture of perseverance, hope in the Lord, and attitudes—powerful strategies to deal with mental blocks.

**Persevere with your children through the block.** Difficult situations have to be faced. As we walk with our children through difficulties, we're helping to develop patience and perseverance and are laying the foundation for life lessons. Lisa was learning the value of hard work and determination, and that mastering concepts takes time and patience.

**Choose your attitudes.** My attitudes affected Lisa's. My frustrations increased hers. My irritation magnified hers. Dealing with the block, I realized, depended on a great extent on how *I* approached it. I could choose frustration, or I could choose joy as we battled through the block.

**Pray with your child.** My daughter was learning that there's nothing too big or small to take to Jesus. He longs to walk beside us through the good and the difficult. Lisa was realizing that her sufficiency comes from Jesus. "I can do everything through him who gives me strength" (Philippians 4:13) has become our school motto.

**Celebrate.** The "aha" moment when Lisa finally "got it" was priceless. We jumped for joy and danced around the room when she was able to work through her math problems without mistakes and angst, and we thanked God for getting us through another round with the block.

**Digging deeper:** Reflect on Deuteronomy 20:4; Psalm 60:11-12.

# When the Going Gets Tough

Let us not become weary in doing good, for at the proper time we will reap a harvest if we do not give up. (Galatians 6:9)

During challenging homeschool moments, we may weary of doing good. Here are some words of encouragement from homeschool graduates to help keep our eyes on the prize.

"I know homeschooling can be challenging—I didn't always make it easy for my mom. However, the trials and difficulties only last for a season, but the harvest lasts a lifetime and beyond. Don't get caught up in the trials of today. Look ahead to where you're going. Press on."—Jonathan Lewis, editor, *Homeschool Enrichment Magazine*

"Know the vision. Form a philosophy of education and concrete goals for your family and your homeschool that go beyond academics. Remember Habakkuk 2:2: 'Then the LORD replied: "Write down the revelation and make it plain on tablets."' Write down your vision and goals. Remind yourself of them. It's not always easy to get through the hard days, but if you don't know why you're getting through them, it's almost impossible."—Rachel Star Thomson, writer and editor

"Your identity and worth are in being a child of God, not in being 'The Perfect Homeschooler.' Allow yourself and your family to be imperfect, and have fun, believing that God is with you and will work all things out for good.

"Remember your purpose. I've highlighted verses in my Bible about passing on my faith to my children and training so I can easily find them during hard days. I have to remember that God is not interested in my rearing academic geniuses or my maintaining a perfect house. He is after my heart and that of my offspring."—Lea Ann Garfias, homeschooling mom of four

**Digging deeper:** On challenging homeschool days, what encourages you to keep homeschooling? Reflect on Deuteronomy 6.

# They'll Get It!

"Be strong and do not give up, for your work
will be rewarded." (2 Chronicles 15:7)

*Pamela Austin, homeschooling mom of three, shares her son's reading journey:*

We love to read. Our first child read by age five. At six, we encouraged Trevor to read, but he didn't *want* to. Halfway through age eight, he read, but it was painful—to hear, and to think our child would never willingly pick up a book and be drawn into another world.

To say I did not shed a few tears, or to deny that my husband and I did not agree on where we should go, would be a lie. Trevor didn't have eye issues nor learning or developmental issues. He knew his letters and could read short chapter books.

When he turned nine, our prayers became desperate. But I told Trevor that God was with him, and he would be fine.

That Thanksgiving, we listened to Mike Lupica's *Heat* on the way to Florida. Trevor begged to listen to it again. Since his sisters didn't agree to, he had to wait until we got home.

I saw the book at a mall and asked Trevor if he'd like a copy. He said, "Sure!" Because the book was 220 pages, I figured Philip and I would be reading it to him.

Trevor started the book when we got home, and finished it four days later. He read it two more times and asked for a similar book, which he read in less than a week. At nine and a half, Trevor was reading, and *loving* it!

It was hard to trust God and not push Trevor. But God was faithful. So, be encouraged when you can't see the results. "Be strong and do not give up, for your work will be rewarded."

**Digging deeper:** Max Elliott Anderson, once a reluctant reader, now writes children's books and offers practical help for reluctant readers at www.maxbooks.9k.com.

*reading resource*

# Living Worthy of the Lord

We continually ask God to fill you with the knowledge
of his will . . . so that you may live a life worthy of the
Lord. (Colossians 1:9-10)

*How can I live a life worthy of the Lord?* I wondered as I read Colossians 1:9-10. As I searched for answers, I discovered Ephesians 4:1: "I urge you to live a life worthy of the calling you have received." With that my question became: *How can I homeschool in a way that is worthy of the Lord?*

The key is revealed through Paul's words in today's passage: "We continually ask God." He then unpacks the contents of that prayer: "to fill you with the knowledge of his will through all the wisdom and understanding that the Spirit gives."

**"We have not stopped praying for you."** Prayer is crucial to homeschooling. It undergirds our school and draws us closer to the heart of God. Prayer shows our children our need for Jesus. On the not-so-easy homeschooling days, constant prayer for wisdom, patience, faithfulness, and discernment is our lifeline.

**"The knowledge of his will"** encompasses every step of our homeschooling journey. It includes discerning God's will to homeschool and what God desires to accomplish through our homeschool. We seek the Lord's will in choosing curricula and activities, discovering our children's strengths and weaknesses, and knowing how to disciple their hearts.

**"Through all the wisdom and understanding that the Spirit gives."** Homeschooling goes beyond acquiring knowledge. We encourage the pursuit of true wisdom, which comes from fearing the Lord (Psalm 111:10). That involves nurturing the hearts of our children and pointing them to Jesus.

**Digging deeper:** How do you encourage the pursuit of true wisdom in your homeschool? Reflect on Colossians 1:3-13.

# Homeschooling Worthy of God's Calling

... and please him in every way: bearing fruit in every good work, growing in the knowledge of God. (Colossians 1:10)

Colossians 1:10 unwraps more ways in which we can homeschool in a manner worthy of the Lord.

**"Please him."** The meaning of "please," I discovered, is about our hearts and our desire to live in a way that honors God.

Homeschooling has many blessings, but its challenges may cause our vulnerabilities—such as doubts, wondering if it's worth it, or even the temptation to give up—to surface. In those moments, our comfort is this: God knows our hearts (1 Kings 8:39). God sees our desire to obey and remain faithful despite our weaknesses.

**"Bearing fruit in every good work."** The fruit of our homeschooling labors is seldom immediate. It may take a few days or months before all the pieces of the learning puzzle fall into place. The blossoming of character takes years of planting the seeds of God's Word and nurturing our children's hearts. But we persist, knowing that in the end God will bring forth a harvest of righteousness.

**"Growing in the knowledge of God."** Homeschooling provides unparalleled opportunities to disciple our children's hearts.

Homeschooling also brings me face-to-face with my shortcomings—my impatience and my tendency to get caught up in schedules and activities, and my proclivity to compare myself with other homeschool parents. When I see the condition of my heart and the areas in which I need God's grace, I long for more of Jesus.

There's nothing quite like homeschooling that keeps me on my knees and reveals God's faithfulness and power. Jesus proves that his grace *is* sufficient for each homeschooling day.

**Digging deeper:** How can you homeschool in a manner worthy of God's calling?

# "But What about Me?"

I urge you to live a life worthy of the calling you have received. . . . Be completely humble. (Ephesians 4:1-2)

"You finished elementary school, today!" Jim smiled at Lisa during dinner. "That calls for a celebration. Which restaurant would you like to go to tomorrow?"

"*Any* restaurant?" Lisa's eyes grew wide. "Longhorn?" She squealed when Jim nodded.

I stared at my plate. *Why couldn't I have a say in where we ate? Hadn't I homeschooled her all these years?*

Jim's voice interrupted my pity party. "And I get to take Mommy out on a date later. It's her celebration too."

My cheeks burned as I studied my plate. *Lord, forgive my selfishness and pride. Help me serve in humility.*

That incident reminded me of my desire to live worthy of my calling to homeschool. According to Ephesians 4:2, being "completely humble" is one step on this journey.

Paul challenges us to have the same attitude as Jesus (Philippians 2:5). Since our attitudes influence our behavior, it's not surprising that humility starts within. Jesus, the Son of God, became our perfect example when he stripped himself of his privileges and rightful dignity (Philippians 2:5-7).

Humility is born out of our utter dependence on and need for God. In the absence of humility, pride gets a foothold. We homeschool out of our own wisdom and abilities rather than in God's strength for *his* glory. Homeschooling is about serving the Lord and our families in humility. Only a heart that is emptied of self can be filled by the Master and poured out in his service.

"Homeschooling is constantly dying to self," a friend commented. I haven't come across a more eloquent, succinct description of homeschooling.

**Digging deeper:** *Lord, more of you and less of me.* Spend some time reflecting on Philippians 2:1-11.

*Good quote*

**24**

# "That's Enough!"

Be completely . . . gentle. (Ephesians 4:2)

"Sleep well." I kissed Katy as she lay down for her afternoon nap.

I stretched out on the sofa downstairs, exhausted from a sleepless night with a fussy baby and from math issues with Lisa. Five minutes later, my ten-month-old's cries filled the house. I pulled myself upstairs and stroked her cheek. "You need to sleep, sweetie."

After forty-five minutes of trudging up and down to her room, I'd had enough. My voice rose with every word, "That's enough, Katy! Lie down and go to sleep."

I stomped downstairs, her voice following me, mimicking my tone and volume perfectly. I snapped at Lisa at the foot of the stairs. "Stop laughing and finish school!"

I blinked back tears. *Lord, what do I do? Katy won't sleep. I'm exhausted. I took it out on both girls.*

"Be completely . . . gentle." Ephesians 4:2, my Bible reading from that morning, etched itself across my mind. *Be gentle? With a stubborn toddler and a preteen who is convinced she doesn't know math?*

*Help me, Lord.* I started up the stairs.

"What's the matter, Katy?" I held her until she calmed down. When I tucked her into bed, my tone was soft but firm. "It's time for a nap." She nodded. Within minutes she was asleep.

After asking Lisa for forgiveness, we laughed together over Katy's imitation of me.

Later I studied the biblical meaning of gentleness. It had nothing to do with weakness but referred to a strength that comes through submission to God. It meant placing my natural inclination to assert myself at Jesus' feet, allowing his rule in my life.

Since then, firmness tempered with gentleness goes a long way in my home and school.

*Lord, through your Holy Spirit, may a gentle and quiet spirit prevail in my home and school.*

**Digging deeper:** How is gentleness evident in your home and school? Reflect on 1 Peter 3:4.

[ Homeschool and You ] **DAY** 25

# "Why Does She Take So Long?"

Be patient. (Ephesians 4:2)

Some days my homeschool mirrors my sin nature. A vicious cycle operates: *Why is she taking so long to finish handwriting? She forgot to tidy the school closet again.* I snap at Lisa despite a voice inside me cautioning, *Step back; don't do it.* When her lower lip trembles, my heart clenches, and I pray, "Lord, I've blown it. You're so patient with me, why can't I be with her? Please forgive me." Even though I ask Lisa for forgiveness, I berate myself. *You need to be more patient.*

On such days, Paul's desperate cry resonates with me: "I do not understand what I do. For what I want to do I do not do, but what I hate I do. . . . I have the desire to do what is good, but I cannot carry it out. . . . The evil I do not want to do—this I keep on doing" (Romans 7:15-19).

When I discovered that the biblical meaning of patience included the sense of enduring, persevering, and not being quick to retaliate, my heart sank. *Lord, how can I ever hope to have that kind of patience?* As I continued my study, hope took hold of my heart when I read Galatians 5:22-23: "But the fruit of the Spirit is love, joy, peace, patience, kindness, goodness, faithfulness, gentleness and self-control."

The Holy Spirit living in me allows the blossoming of a supernatural patience with my children and myself. As I continue to allow the Holy Spirit to work in me, I will be able to "correct, rebuke and encourage—with great patience and careful instruction" (2 Timothy 4:2).

**Digging deeper:** Reflect on 1 Corinthians 13:4.

[ Homeschool and Family ] **DAY** 26

# "But She's Annoying"

. . . bearing with one another in love. (Ephesians 4:2)

"Mama." Lisa, then seven years old, broke my concentration as I checked her grammar workbook. "Remember the girl we met the other day? Well, I think she's annoying."

I looked at her. "Do you think Jesus loves her?" She hesitated then nodded slightly. "What do you think Jesus would want you to do?"

She sighed. "Be her friend."

That incident reminded me of Ephesians 4:2. "Bearing" can also mean "showing tolerance for one another" (NASB) and "making allowance for each other's faults" (NLT).

In homeschooling the masks come off—parent and child see each other as we really are. At times our perspectives and idiosyncrasies may wear on others. (Even, and perhaps especially, in families it's not always easy to bear with one another.)

Yet the Bible encourages us to do just that. It doesn't mean overlooking sin but respecting one another because we are each made in the image of God. We don't always have to agree. We can disagree with grace.

How is this possible? The rest of Ephesians 4:2 gives the answer—because of love. Jesus declared, "A new command I give you: Love one another. As I have loved you, so you must love one another" (John 13:34). John makes a thought-provoking statement: "Anyone who does not love their brother and sister, whom they have seen, cannot love God, whom they have not

**27**

seen" (1 John 4:20). We can bear with each other when God's perfect love overflows from our hearts.

*Lord, help us to be channels of your perfect love.*

**Digging deeper:** Reflect on 1 John 3:11-24; 4:7-21.


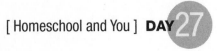

[ Homeschool and You ]  **DAY** 27

# Mending Fences

Make every effort to keep the unity of the Spirit
through the bond of peace. (Ephesians 4:3)


"Where are your calculations for the problems?"

Ten-year-old Lisa pointed to a few scribbles in her math book.

"That's not enough. I've told you before that I need to see each step."

She shrugged. "I like to do it in my head."

"But that's how you make mistakes. I want to know where you go wrong so I can help." I pushed the papers across the table. "Redo them the way I've told you to."

"This is so *not* fair! It'll take me all afternoon."

"You should've thought about that before you handed me unacceptable work. You need to obey even when it doesn't make sense to you." My voice rose.

"Th–this is the only reason I d–don't like homeschooling." Lisa's sobs punctuated each word. "Sometimes when you get mad at school, it follows us all day."

Each word hit hard. She was right in this case. I was being hard on her at school because she had messed up at home earlier. Blinking back tears, I left the room.

"Lord," I said as I sank onto the sofa, "you know I try to keep home issues and school issues separate, but I messed up. Forgive me. Please help me."

I flipped to Ephesians 4:3. The words "alert at noticing differences and quick at mending fences" (MSG) jumped off the page.

Though the boundaries between home and school may blur, I can be quick to mend fences.

As I went in search of Lisa, we almost collided.

"Mom." She twisted a strand of hair. "Um, you don't *always* let things in school follow us through the day."

"I'm sorry, too, sweetie." We hugged.

**Digging deeper:** How do you separate home and school issues? Reflect on Colossians 3:12-15.

[ Gifts We Give Our Children ] **DAY** 28

# A Godly Heritage

I will sing of the LORD's great love forever;
with my mouth I will make your faithfulness
known through all generations. (Psalm 89:1)

Devotions were a must at my grandparents' home. As a child, I was excused from the morning sessions but not the night ones.

When the ancient clock on the white living room wall struck nine every night, no matter who was visiting or what was happening, we gathered in the living room. A hush descended as the women, in reverence, covered their bowed heads with the edge of their *saris*. After my grandmother handed out tattered hymn books, she sank onto the wicker sofa's thin cushion.

My grandfather's gnarled, bony hands, trembling now and then, caressed the worn leather of his Bible that rested on his lap. After a few hymns, he'd lift the Bible close to his eyes and read, his voice quavering with emotion now and then.

I stared out the window at the flickers of brightness as fireflies zigzagged through the darkness. I wondered how soon I could get back to the stack of books that beckoned me. Most often I nodded off on my mother's lap during prayers.

As a child I never imagined that those devotional times would later spark a hunger in me for the Lord. As I grew up, the power of those memories went a long way in helping me to develop spiritual disciplines.

My grandparents' commitment to daily seek the Lord, no matter what, encourages me to pass that heritage on to my children. As Jim and I disciple our children, I rest in the hope that the seeds sown during our family devotional times will one day reap a harvest of righteousness.

**Digging deeper:** How do you pass on a godly heritage to your children? Reflect on Deuteronomy 4:1-13.

[ Homeschool Foundations ] **DAY** 29

# Custom-made Journeys

So God created mankind in his own image.
(Genesis 1:27)

As a child growing up in India, I loved the adventure of getting new clothes. Within minutes of stepping into the fabric store, organza, silks, and cottons of various patterns and hues draped the counters as the owner unraveled yards of each fabric that caught our eye. My grandmother took her time making her selections.

At the tailor's she poured over patterns, choosing each outfit with care to suit the occasion—casual, church, parties, or weddings. Once my measurements were taken under her watchful eye, we'd leave with the promise of the garments being ready "soon."

The day the outfits were delivered, I twirled around in each one, my grandmother's voice in the background, "Take the hem up a bit." "We need a tuck here." By the time the alterations were done, each outfit fit perfectly.

When I start each new school year, I remember the meticulous care that went into tailoring custom clothing. I'm awed and humbled that the God who spoke the world into being and took time to fashion each person guides me. Along the way when I'm tempted to compare our homeschool to others' homeschools, I can rest in the fact that just as God created each human being to be unique, the education he weaves for my children and the choices he's led my husband and me to make will be a perfect fit.

**Digging deeper:** How does knowing that God guides your homeschooling decisions help you?

# Encouragement on Your Journey

*support groups*

Let us consider how we may spur one another on toward love and good deeds, not giving up meeting together . . . but encouraging one another. (Hebrews 10:24-25)

*What's a homeschool support meeting?* I wondered as I checked my e-mail.

When we moved to Atlanta, I was amazed at the opportunities that a larger homeschool group offered. So after homeschooling for four years, I attended my first homeschool support meeting.

I never realized, until I stepped into that group of warm, welcoming parents, how much I had needed a "safe place" to share my homeschooling joys and frustrations.

It's been five years since that meeting, and now those meetings are a vital part of my homeschooling journey. They are Hebrews 10:24-25 in action.

- There's something special about being with parents who understand the homeschooling life. I'm comforted that my child isn't the only one whose eyes glaze over at math or who forgets chores.

- I have hope when I hear how others got through difficult homeschool moments.
- I'm spurred on to continue nurturing my children's hearts and follow God's leading.
- I learn from parents on a wide variety of topics—homeschooling, parenting, marriage, and spiritual issues.
- We pray for and with each other. When iritis attacked my eyes while writing this book, the group undergirded me with prayer.
- We are there for each other. A mom recently shared her story of financial devastation. The group contributed money toward her family's rent.
- Support groups for only children, middle school and high school kids, and children with special needs provide specialized help for families.

I leave each meeting grateful for the privilege of being with parents who freely give of themselves to others.

**Digging deeper:** When was the last time you attended a homeschool support group? Prayerfully consider starting one if there is no such group where you live.

[ Homeschool and You ] **DAY** 31

# Missing Out?

Surely everyone goes around like a mere phantom;
in vain they rush about. (Psalm 39:6)

January 12, 2007. Washington, DC. Strains of some of the world's best classical music filled L'Enfant Plaza station for about forty-five minutes during the early morning rush hour.

Who was the musician? None other than one-time child prodigy, now one of the world's premier violinists, Joshua Bell, playing his $3.5 million Stradivarius violin.

Why would someone of his caliber perform in a metro station? The *Washington Post* arranged his performance as an "experiment in context, perception and priorities." Would people stop to appreciate beauty in the midst of their daily rush? Unaware of the violinist's identity, only 7 of the 1,097 commuters stopped to listen.

Why didn't more people stop? They didn't have time.

I'm all too familiar with the feeling of being rushed as I keep up with my responsibilities. Some days it seems like I rush about "in vain." Despite my frenetic pace, I don't feel like I've accomplished much at the end of those days.

Gene Weingartent pointed out, "If we can't take the time out of our lives to stay a moment and listen to one of the best musicians on earth play some of the best music ever written; if the surge of modern life so overpowers us that we are deaf and blind to something like that—then what else are we missing?"*

**Digging deeper:** Are you missing out on anything in your effort to get to everything scheduled each day? Reflect on Psalm 39.

*Gene Weingarten, "Pearls before Breakfast," *Washington Post*, April 8, 2007, http://www.washingtonpost.com/wp-dyn/content/article/2007/04/04/AR2007040401721.html.

[ Homeschool and You ] **DAY** 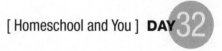32

# Being Busy or Prioritizing?

Teach us to number our days, that we may gain a heart of wisdom. (Psalm 90:12)

What was I missing out on in my rush to get things done each day? Was being busy robbing me of special times with my family? What about opportunities to reach out to others? Was there a balance? These questions swirled around in my mind after I read the *Washington Post*'s report.

One morning the message of Psalm 90:12 brought things into perspective. In essence, the psalmist asked God to help him remember the fleeting nature of life so he would be prudent in the way he lived. I, too, realized I needed to put important things first.

"My days on earth are few, Lord. I want every one of them to count. Help me live wisely," I prayed as I ended my devotional time.

In the following weeks, I prayed through three questions:

1. Given my to-do lists and schedules, what is important in the light of eternity?
2. Does everything on my list *have* to get done?
3. Do the activities and to-do lists reflect God's heart for my family and me?

Then I had to do what needed to be done: cut back on various areas of involvement as I felt the Lord leading and make a conscious effort to pray before taking on new commitments. As I learn to number my days, I'm discovering the need for flexibility. Priorities can change depending on circumstances, so I try to revisit my list and schedules every four to six months.

The psalmist's prayer, "Teach us to number our days," is a step toward wise living.

**Digging deeper:** Are you busy, or do you prioritize? Reflect on Psalm 90.

# Organizing

Everything should be done in a fitting and
orderly way. (1 Corinthians 14:40)

"Mom, where's the handwriting paper?"

I closed my eyes and bit my lower lip. *Not again.* "It's in the school closet."

Ten-year-old Lisa's head popped around the door with a sheepish grin. "Sorry, I forgot."

We were having a hard time adjusting to doing school in the kitchen. With the additions to our family—my mother living with us and our new baby—we no longer had the luxury of a schoolroom and all the storage it provided.

*How hard is it to put things in their places?* I wondered a few days later when I couldn't find the construction paper again. I'm not super organized, but I like knowing where things are and what is scheduled for each day. So I decided it was time to take action.

After some brainstorming to find more storage space, Jim turned a coat closet into the school closet. I then labeled boxes and file folders, making sure Lisa knew where everything went. As long as things were put away in a somewhat neat fashion every day, I was happy.

I made sure Lisa knew and understood what was expected of her: Completed daily school assignments were to be placed in a folder on the dining table by 3:00 every afternoon. After I reviewed them, she was responsible for filing them in each subject folder.

Every Sunday my to-do list for school, personal/home, and business helped me prioritize and spread tasks over the week.

Organization is helping me be a better steward of time and resources. It focuses me and gives me peace along with a sense of accomplishment.

**Digging deeper:** Visit www.flylady.net for organizing tips.

# Time Management

Make the most of every opportunity. (Colossians 4:5)

"I wish there were more than twenty-four hours in the day." My friend's voice crackled over the phone as she did errands between swim team practices and piano classes. I knew the feeling.

*How can I fit in school, home, activities, Bible study, devotions, writing, and social time without going crazy?* I often wonder. I'm not there yet, but the following principles guide me:

- I pray for sensitivity to the needs of my family, open eyes for teachable moments, flexibility to go with the flow of life, and blessings on the time God has given us.
- A set time for school allows our family to better plan our activities, free time, and social time.
- To minimize distractions and my stress level, I avoid multi-tasking during school.
- A master calendar and school schedule posted in a central place help me keep track of our commitments.
- Though we have set times for each subject, I make sure our school day allows for extra time in subjects if needed.
- I set aside a few minutes of fun downtime each day with my children.
- I factor in time for the unexpected.
- I try to pray before taking on new commitments.

Grace and flexibility undergird everything. I don't want to be so focused on getting things done that I'm blind to opportunities to make memories and nurture the hearts of my children.

**Digging deeper:** Where does most of your time go?

# Marriage and Homeschooling

Do not withhold good from those to whom it is due,
when it is in your power to act. (Proverbs 3:27)

Parents relaxed around the fireplace sipping coffee during our monthly homeschool encouragement meeting. The glow of the lamps and the flickering candles softened the topic—being a spouse in the midst of busy homeschool lives. All, without exception, admitted that finding a balance in this area wasn't easy.

"Why do our spouses get the short end of the stick?" asked one mom. Heads nodded. "I'm busy during the day with school, kids, activities, and housework. After supper, when the kids are in bed, I want to take some time for myself, but it's hard, because that's the only time my husband and I have together."

"I want to feel more like a wife rather than only a mom," said another parent.

We shared solutions:

- Get away with your spouse. "If you have the chance, take it," urged a veteran homeschool mom with teenagers. "I know it's hard, but it'll do the relationship a world of good."
- Be proactive about scheduling kid-free time with your spouse.
- Ask your spouse what you can do to make him or her feel important to you.
- Pace yourself. "I'm careful about how much energy I spend during the day so that when my husband comes home, I'm not exhausted," another mom offered.
- Ask for help. In general, spouses would rather take on additional household tasks than to have a stressed, exhausted partner.
- Prioritize tasks and spread them through the week to better balance responsibilities.

**Digging deeper:** Surprise your spouse with a date.

I think she gets it. 'Time alone with the Lord' is really every moment of every day.

# Time for the Lord

Jesus often withdrew to lonely places and prayed.
(Luke 5:16)

Three-month-old Katy's cries roused me. I had dozed off again while reading my Bible. *I'll finish my quiet time later. Jesus, God incarnate, withdrew to connect with the Father, so how much more I need to. But how and when?* I wondered as I pulled myself out of bed. Since Katy's birth, finding uninterrupted time for my devotions when I wasn't tired was a challenge.

A few days later, during another bout when nothing I did could calm my crying baby, I slid a worship CD into the player. The music soothed her and helped me focus on the Lord, refreshing me. Scripture set to music stayed with me through the day—a balm to my soul.

Maybe it didn't matter so much how I spent my time with Jesus each day, as long as I met with him daily. The thought renewed and excited me.

In the following days, instead of having my quiet time first thing in the morning, I read my Bible when I was more awake—during ten-year-old Lisa's self-directed study time. I reflected on those verses during my day.

Short intervals during the day offered windows of prayer time. "Thanks for Jim and all he does for us," I whispered as I folded laundry. "Draw my girls to you at an early age, Lord," I prayed while changing a diaper. "Thanks for this house—for heat and air conditioning," I said as I cleaned.

As the months passed, those little windows of time kept me focused on the Lord throughout the day. I found myself spiritually reenergized. It *was* possible to spend time with the Lord in this new phase of my life. I had found a new normal.

**Digging deeper:** When and how do you meet with the Lord? Reflect on John 15:1-8.

# Time for Yourself

Do you not know that your bodies are temples
of the Holy Spirit? (1 Corinthians 6:19)

"You need to take time for yourself." My OB/GYN drummed his fingers on the counter as he sat across from me at my six-month postpartum check-up.

I shrugged. *Easier said than done. You don't homeschool. You don't have a baby who doesn't like to sleep; nor are you caregiver to an aging mother.*

"Unless you're rested, you can't be any good to your family." *He's right.* Many days I was close to tears, irritable and over-whelmed. Yet I longed to enjoy my family.

I recharge by being alone. Without a few minutes of "alone" time, I feel drained emotionally. But how could I take time for myself when my family needed me?

My doctor pulled his chair closer and met my gaze. "Find something you like doing. Do that for a half hour every day—guilt-free. Indulge yourself. That's an order."

Jim encouraged me to take a few minutes every day to listen to classical music or read, and gave me a few hours of alone time on weekends. But it didn't hit home until 1 Corinthians 6:19 sank into my heart. I am a temple of the living God! Part of my stewardship is to take care of myself physically—a healthy diet, rest, exercise, time to unwind—so I can better serve my family. I've found that when I take care of myself and am rested, life is more enjoyable and my joy in homeschooling and serving my family soars.

**Digging deeper:** What do you do to take care of yourself? Carve out twenty to thirty minutes this week to do something *you* enjoy.

*I wonder what Amy Carmichael would say about this...*

**39**

# "Let Her Fail!"

The one who loves their children is careful
to discipline them. (Proverbs 13:24)

"You have a social studies test tomorrow," I reminded Lisa, then
in fifth grade.

She nodded, and continued reading a novel.

"Are you prepared?

"I did the unit review."

"That's not enough. You need to study the chapters."

The rest of the day came and went. Her social studies textbook
remained untouched.

"Let her fail," Jim advised when I told him what had happened.

"I can't do that!"

"You're not doing her any favors if you don't."

*Maybe I should give her another day to prepare. Would that happen
in school? You know Jim is right.* I argued with myself as I struggled
with not wanting to let her fail and knowing the right thing to do.

"It's not about you." Jim reached for my hand. "You're not a
bad mother or teacher if she fails. It's about discipline and letting
her learn a lesson."

"Thank you, Lord, for a wise husband," I murmured as the
truth penetrated my heart.

The Bible has much to say about discipline. God disciplines us
for our good—to develop character and to set us on the path of
holy living. In fact, "the Lord disciplines the one he loves"
(Hebrews 12:6). It's because we love our children that we help them
learn and grow from their mistakes. Proverbs encourages parents to
discipline their children, for "in that there is hope" (19:18).

*Lord, thank you for reminding me that I'm preparing my children for
life by allowing them to face and learn from the consequences of their
mistakes. Help me to know when and how to discipline.*

**Digging deeper:** Do you find it hard to let your children fail? Why
or why not? Reflect on Hebrews 12:7-11.

*Good question.*

**40**

# Learning from failure

No discipline seems pleasant at the time, but painful. Later
on, however, it produces a harvest of righteousness and peace
for those who have been trained by it. (Hebrews 12:11)

"Are you ready for your social studies assessment?"

Lisa nodded. I bit my lower lip to keep from asking, "Are you
sure?"

I brought up her online assessment and left the room.

About half an hour later, I ran back in at the sound of loud
sobs. She sat at the desk, her head buried in her arms.

Lisa lifted her tear-streaked face when I placed my hand on her
shoulder. "I—I failed," she hiccupped through sobs. On the screen
I read, "You scored 60 percent. You need to review the unit."

I bent down and put my arms around her, my heart clenching.
*Lord, this is so hard.*

Later that night, a curly head peeked around my bedroom
door.

I looked up from my book and smiled. She entered and stood
by the side of my bed, twisting her hands. "I'm sorry. I didn't listen to you and study."

We hugged.

Discipline is painful for both the giver and receiver. But
Hebrews points out that "it produces a harvest of righteousness
and peace for those who have been trained by it." Discipline is a
large part of training our children and helps to point them in the
right direction.

Both of us came away from that experience richer. More often
than not, Lisa is more serious about preparing for assessments.
I'm learning when it's in her best interest to protect her and when
it's not.

**Digging deeper:** Think about a time when discipline, though
painful for you to give, benefited your children. Reflect on
Proverbs 3:11-12 and 29:17.

# Upside-Down Kingdom Principles

Then he said to them all: "Whoever wants to be my disciple must deny themselves and take up their cross daily and follow me." (Luke 9:23)

Deny oneself in a culture of self-indulgence?

Jesus said, "Anyone who wants to be first must be the very last, and the servant of all" (Mark 9:35). How does that work in a "me-first culture"?

How can a meek person inherit the earth (Matthew 5:5)? How does one rejoice in the face of persecution, insults, and false accusations (vv. 10-12)?

How could Paul, Jesus' follower, be content in want or hunger (Philippians 4:12)? How does that apply to us in a culture of abundance?

What prompted many of Jesus' followers to endure unimaginable torture for the sake of a person in whom they believed, whom some hadn't even seen (Hebrews 11:36-37)?

The one who inspired such faith and devotion bids us live by the upside-down principles of his kingdom—values that defy logic and run counter to the world in which we live.

How can we help our children internalize these values?

- Live them. Homeschooling gives our children opportunities to see us live by kingdom values.
- Be honest when we stumble. Our frailties reveal the power of the cross.
- Talk about our values. Articulate and explain kingdom values and their importance to us.
- Give our children opportunities to live out kingdom values.
- Answer their questions without getting defensive.

The King of Kings and Lord of Lords who took on humanity and was born in a cattle stall, the one who washed his disciples' feet and who died that we might live has left us an example that we might follow in his steps and encourage our children to do so as well.

**Digging deeper:** Reflect on Matthew 5:1-12. Read *The Jesus Style* by Gayle D. Erwin.

# Exceeding Expectations?

Hope deferred makes the heart sick, but a longing fulfilled is a tree of life. (Proverbs 13:12)

"Congratulations!" I yelled as I scanned nine-year-old Lisa's writing test results. I put the paper on the kitchen island and grabbed her hand to dance around the kitchen, but she reached for the paper.

"Man, I wanted to get 'exceed expectations,' Mommy." Her voice quivered and tears filled her eyes.

"But you did well, sweetie," I drew her into my arms. Thoughts ran through my mind as I held her until her sobs subsided. *Did I communicate unrealistic expectations of her? It's good that she has high goals. How do I help her deal with disappointment and develop realistic expectations?*

We're familiar with the dull ache when things don't work out the way we would have liked. "Hope deferred makes the heart sick," says Proverbs 13:12. The root meaning of the word *sick* ranges from diseased and weakened to hurt. Unfulfilled longings or expectations weaken us, cause self-doubts, drain our ability to go on, and make us sick at heart.

Since encouraging my children to develop realistic expectations starts with me, I consider the following questions:

- What do I expect of my children? Are those expectations reasonable for their ages and maturity levels?
- Have I communicated high expectations and performance-based love?
- How realistic is it to expect more of my children?

These questions make me more aware of my expectations and provide the starting point for a conversation with Lisa. Then I can help her find her level and develop realistic expectations and goals. As she takes tiny steps toward meeting those goals, she is encouraged and her confidence is restored. She receives life and hope.

**Digging deeper:** What are your expectations of your children?

[ Homeschool Basics ] **DAY**

# Do Your Best

Whatever you do, work at it with all your heart, as working
for the Lord, not for human masters. (Colossians 3:23)

"You didn't make it." My French professor pointed to me. A cold shiver ran down my spine. At age nineteen, it was the first time I hadn't passed a French test. "But if you do very well in tomorrow's orals, you have hope." He moved on to the next student.

The rest of my two-hour Business French postgraduate class passed in a blur.

By the time I dragged myself home, I was sick to my stomach. That night my father came into my room and sat on the edge of my bed.

"I know you're upset," he said to my back as I lay facing the wall. "Did you do your best?"

At my nod, I felt a soft pat on my shoulder.

"Good, that's all I need to know."

I turned toward him. "You mean you're not upset with me?"

"Why? I saw how much you studied. You did your best. That's what's important."

I sat up and searched his eyes.

He held my hand. "Always do your best for God. Not for me or anyone else. Then you won't be ashamed." I heard his voice as he shut the door to my room, "Give your orals your best shot."

The next day my professor looked at me and said, "Your oral exam was one of the best in the class."

The relief at getting my certification in French has long since faded. But my father's words, echoing Scripture, have stayed with me. "Whatever you do, work at it with all your heart, as working for the Lord, not for human masters."

**Digging deeper:** Toward what goal do you motivate your children? Reflect on Colossians 3:22-24.

[ Homeschool and Family ] **DAY** 43

# "I Wanted to Chat"

May the words of my mouth and this meditation of my heart be pleasing in your sight, LORD, my Rock and my Redeemer. (Psalm 19:14)

Jim sank onto the sofa with a bowl of popcorn. His hand hovered over the TV remote. Then he glanced at me. "How was your day?"

"Okay. And yours?"

"Good."

The crunch of popcorn broke the silence in the room.

After several minutes, he clicked the TV remote.

"Jim, I wanted to chat."

"Anita! I've been waiting for you to chat. I even tried to get the conversation going." His voice rose as he tossed the remote on the sofa.

"Fine. Watch your TV show!" I stomped off. "I was trying to give you time to unwind," I snapped, halfway up the stairs.

Expectations impact relationships. They influence how we perceive and respond to others. It's only when things don't work out the way we think they should that we become aware of our own expectations, which are subconscious and, many times, unrealistic. That night I wanted to chat but thought Jim would appreciate some time to relax. He wanted to watch TV but thought he was giving me a chance to chat. In both cases, our expectations of each other were not met, causing misunderstanding. To avoid situations like these, we try to:

- Be honest about our expectations—both of ourselves and each other. But honesty comes only through prayerful introspection: "Test me, LORD, and try me, examine my heart and my mind" (Psalm 26:2).
- Be willing to share our expectations with each other in an accepting atmosphere and prayerfully find a balance. "Love . . . rejoices with the truth" (1 Corinthians 13:6).

**Digging deeper:** How do your expectations impact your relationships with your family? Reflect on 1 Corinthians 13.

[ Homeschool and You ]  **DAY** 44

# Supermom?

"Then you will know the truth, and the truth will set you free." (John 8:32)

"Why are you so frazzled these days?" Jim met my gaze over the rim of his glasses.

I almost choked on my latté. My delight at having time alone with him evaporated.

"You're like a tightly coiled spring."

I glared. "I'm just trying to keep up with everything I'm supposed to do."

"Like what?"

I shrugged. "Cooking; cleaning; grocery shopping; taking care of the kids, you, my mom; and homeschooling . . ."

"You're *supposed* to do all that? Says who?"

I paused as his words hit home. "Says me."

His eyes twinkled. "Lower your expectations of yourself. Let the rest of the family pitch in. I'll help, too."

*Could it be that simple?*

He rattled off what he was willing to do and what we could add to Lisa's chore list.

*It's worth a shot,* I thought as we left Starbucks.

In the following weeks, I struggled to let go of my expectations of myself and how things should be done. When Lisa whizzed by sock-skating to clean my floors, I bit my tongue. When eighteen-month-old Katy grabbed a washcloth to clean the floor, I sat on my hands to keep from pulling it away from her. When my mother took double the time than I would to cook a meal, I left the kitchen.

My family didn't care if the banisters were polished every week or if the floor was shining. They were happy with a fairly neat house. My family wasn't interested in elaborate meals, and when we had company, simple meals were fine.

They wanted *me*—a happy, not-so-tired Anita. That truth is setting me free.

**Digging deeper:** What expectations do you have of yourself? Reflect on John 8:31-36.

# Take Off Your Glasses!

Love is kind. . . . It does not dishonor others.
(1 Corinthians 13:4-5)

"I can't believe you haven't commented on the clutter yet," Jim said as we put our suitcases in the closet of our accommodations for the night. I had lost track of the number of house-hunting trips we had made to Atlanta. This time, through some quirky circumstances, we had ended up at an older hotel whose décor wasn't quite my style.

"What's gotten in to you?" he joked. As I turned to face him, I glanced in the mirror, and the reason I hadn't noticed the dust was clear. I didn't have on my glasses.

Several weeks later, eight-year-old Lisa set her weekly hand-writing assignment on my desk. I noticed loops outside the lines. *Will she ever learn to stay in the lines?* I wondered. Some of the *t*s were askew. Several letters slanted in different directions. She had colored outside the outline of the birds in a few places.

As I held the paper up and opened my mouth, a gentle whisper settled in my heart, *Child, take off your glasses!* I swallowed hard and cleared my throat. Lisa bounded across to me.

"Did you like it, Mama? I made it for you." The paper in my hand shook as I put it on the desk and drew her into my arms. "It's beautiful, sweetie. Thank you for thinking of me."

Love is kind and does not dishonor others. In my quest for excellence in schoolwork, I may crush my child's spirit rather than look at the effort she made. But love has a different perspective. I can let the lenses of criticism and perfectionism color my view or look through the lenses of love.

**Digging deeper:** Through which glasses do you look?

# "But I Want to Go to School!"

Pursue righteousness, godliness, faith, love,
endurance and gentleness. Fight the good
fight of the faith. (1 Timothy 6:11-12)

"Why can't I go to school?" Seven-year-old Angel glared at her
mother. "All my friends go to school. They have *fun*."

"Honey, we're doing what God wants us to do. Sometimes
that means being different."

"I don't want to be different. I *want* to go to school!" Angel
stomped off to her room.

She complained about schoolwork, dawdled at meals, and hid
her books. Anne Marie and her husband talked to Angel, tried to
find more homeschooling friends for her, even allowed her to
choose which subject she wanted to start her school day with,
and disciplined her.

They prayed and did character studies. Angel didn't budge.
Anne Marie's desperation grew as did her doubts. *Am I supposed
to homeschool? Why am I sitting here bantering with Angel? If I put
her on the school bus, I'll have time to do what I want to.*

As she grappled with the situation, the word "pursue" in
1 Timothy 6:11 brought everything into perspective. "I had to
pursue God's plan for our lives and not give up. When I
embraced that, God's grace began to transform *me*. I became
more sensitive to Angel and her needs. I didn't cut her off; I listened to her and tried to understand why school and riding the
bus fascinated her so much."

Angel's parents invited her to pray with them about school
options. Two years later they found a solution. Angel entered a
hybrid school. The twice-a-week homeschool classes satisfied
both Anne Marie and Angel.

"We still have our challenges," Anne Marie commented, "but my perspective has changed. Fighting the good fight of faith is well worth it."

**Digging deeper:** How can 1 Timothy 6:11-12 apply to your homeschool?

# Comparisons

The Sovereign LORD is my strength; he makes
my feet like the feet of a deer, he enables me
to go on the heights. (Habakkuk 3:19)

*I'm not as creative as she is. I don't do as much with my kids. How does she manage so many activities?* Thoughts preyed on my mind as I drove away from a homeschool co-op planning meeting. By the time I pulled into our driveway, my sense of inadequacy was at its height. *Would my kids be better served in school?*

"Stop comparing yourself with others," my husband chided when I confided in him. "You do a great job."

"You're just biased," I retorted, and trudged off to a homeschool encouragement meeting. Surprised and relieved, I discovered that I wasn't the only mom who felt she had missed the mark when compared to others.

Comparisons set a vicious cycle in motion. They prey on my insecurities and inadequacies, leading to doubts. I get touchy, and my homeschool isn't at its best.

Several weeks later, as I read from the Amplified Bible, peace took hold of my heart with each word of Habakkuk 3:19: "The Lord God is my Strength, my personal bravery, and my invincible army; He makes my feet like hinds' feet and will make me to walk [not to stand still in terror, but to walk] and make [spiritual] progress upon my high places [of trouble, suffering, or responsibility]!"

I dropped to my knees. "Lord, you are my strength. Please make up whatever is lacking in me so I can be the teacher my children need. Thank you that you will make me surefooted on this path and give progress on the high places of my homeschooling responsibilities."

*Amen!*

**Digging deeper:** How do comparisons affect you? Reflect on 1 Samuel 18.

[ Homeschool and You ] **DAY** 48

# Attitudes

As water reflects the face, so one's life reflects the heart. (Proverbs 27:19)

"Attitudes are everything." My father peered at me over his glasses. "Remember that."

I fixed my eyes on a spot over his head, my teenaged mind on other things. "Yes, Daddy." The truth of his words sank in many years later.

Our attitudes permeate our lives, families, and homeschool. According to Proverbs 27:19, our actions reflect our attitudes. To my frustration, my sin nature often influences my behavior, leading me to desire what is contrary to the Spirit, so that often I don't act in the way I want to (Galatians 5:17).

How can I change my attitudes? By renewing my mind (Romans 12:2).

The constant renewal of my mind, which transforms my attitudes, comes only through spending time in God's Word. Paul encourages us to "think about" things that are true, noble, right, pure, lovely, and admirable (Philippians 4:8)—attributes of God's Word. Memorizing Scripture, listening to praise music, being careful about what I read and listen to, and thinking about God's Word allow truth to seep into my heart. His Word "judges the thoughts and attitudes of the heart" (Hebrews 4:12) and gives me wisdom to make godly choices and decisions, guiding me into right living.

I "take captive every thought to make it obedient to Christ" (2 Corinthians 10:5). Since my attitudes influence my thoughts and behavior, I have to be conscious about allowing God's rule over my mind daily. I ask God to fill me with thoughts that honor him.

When my sin nature gets the better of me and I fail, I go to the cross for mercy. Jesus knows my weaknesses and is ready to give me a clean heart (Psalm 51:7).

**Digging deeper:** How do you renew your mind?

# Fun

There is a time for everything . . . a time to weep
and a time to laugh. (Ecclesiastes 3:1,4)

"Anita, you need to have some fun!" one of the women in my writers' critique group commented. "Go home, take your girls out, and enjoy yourself."

She was right. It had been a while since we'd had silly joke or pajama day. My focus on getting things done made school intense.

The next afternoon, my kids and I headed to a park. "More, more," screamed Katy as the breeze ruffled her hair. She bounced in her stroller, kicking her legs, while Lisa and I chatted as we walked around the park.

"That was fun. We should do this more often," Lisa commented on our way home after Italian ices. I agreed. Just taking an hour away had relaxed us.

When Lisa was younger, it seemed easier to make learning fun and to include fun in our school day. We played math games, sang geography songs, and took a break for a walk or to window shop at the mall. Science experiments that didn't turn out the way they should have brought us much laughter. But nothing matched our all-time favorite: after we read a classic together, our family room became our personal theater as we sat with bowls of popcorn, watching the book come alive in movie form.

Fun, in whatever form, made school more enjoyable and helped us connect. Now, in middle school, we worked hard to get through curricula and make it to activities on time, leaving little time for fun. But the Bible is right—there is a time for everything.

*Help me, Lord, to make time for fun and laughter.*

**Digging deeper:** When was the last time your family had fun in school? Plan something fun this week.

[ And a Child Will Lead Them ] **DAY** 50

# A Child's Perspective

At that time Jesus said, "I praise you, Father, Lord of heaven and earth, because you have hidden these things from the wise and learned, and revealed them to little children." Matthew 11:25

"Mama?" Six-year-old Lisa's voice sliced through my thoughts as we left church.

"Where's Miss Lilly's son?"

My mind was still reeling from the news our pastor had shared with us.

"Mama!" A tug on my hand jerked me back to reality.

"Oh. . . . Sorry, sweetie. He's in jail."

"What's going to happen to him?"

I felt like my blood would boil at the thought of what he had done. "He'll probably stay there for a while."

She was silent all the way home.

Over lunch, my husband and I discussed how we could help the eighty-year-old widow who had taken in her estranged son when he told her Jesus had changed his life. Within a few months, he had stolen her identity, wiped out her bank account, and left her with debt larger than Mount Everest.

"Is he okay in jail?" Lisa's voice interrupted us. Not quite sure what she was getting at, I continued eating.

She broke the silence again. "I'm going to pray for him now."

My head whipped around. "You mean you're going to pray for *Miss Lilly*."

Her brown eyes pinned mine. "No, Mama, her son."

I searched her eyes. "Do you understand what he did to her?"

She nodded. "Mama, Miss Lilly's fine. She knows Jesus." Her voice rose with urgency. "But her son's in jail. He *needs* Jesus." Her words stung.

I didn't hear her prayer. I was busy praying through my own attitudes and emotions.

**Digging deeper:** When has God spoken to you through your child?

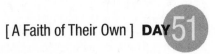

[ A Faith of Their Own ] **DAY** 51

# "How Do I Know It's True?"

"But what about you?" he asked. "Who do you say I am?"
Peter answered, "You are the Messiah." (Mark 8:29)

"Mama, how do I know that what I believe is true?" My fingers froze on the dry erase board. I turned around, willing myself to stay calm.

"What do you mean?"

"Well, I believe in Jesus, but how do I know it's true?"

*Where is this coming from, Lord? Were the eight years of devotions, church, and teaching her about you a waste?*

"Mama?" Lisa's voice interrupted my thoughts.

I put my arm around her. "I can tell you what Jesus has done for me. We can study the evidence proving that Jesus walked this earth. But you have to believe for yourself. I can't do that for you." Our discussion that day was one of many on her faith journey.

In the following days, worry and gratitude pulled me in opposite directions. *Hadn't she been baptized on profession of faith? At least this happened while she was still home. I'm glad she shared her questions with me.*

Mark 8:27-29 became my solace. When Jesus asked his disciples who people said he was, they answered, "Some say John the Baptist; others say Elijah; and still others, one of the prophets." But Jesus pressed further, more interested in who *they* declared him to be. Acknowledging Jesus as the Christ only comes through personal faith (1 John 4:15).

Jesus' question comforted me. He was concerned about my daughter's faith, wanting it to become personal. She had begun her pilgrimage toward truth. Jesus was in control.

*Thank you, Lord, that you want my children to know you. Open their eyes to who you are and lead them to faith in you.*

**Digging deeper:** What reassurance does Mark 8:27-29 offer you?

[ A Faith of Their Own ] **DAY**  52

# Handling Questions about faith

But as for you, continue in what you have learned
and have become convinced of, because you know
those from whom you learned it. (2 Timothy 3:14)

*Was my child alone in questioning her faith?* Unsure, I researched faith in young people. A Barna study of eight- to twelve-year-olds showed that "overall, less than four out of every ten young people (38 percent) said that churches have made a positive difference in their life. An even smaller number (34 percent) said that prayer is very important to them."* The study observed that kids experience changes and significant challenges between ages eleven and thirteen, a time when their self-image is in flux and they are making increasingly independent decisions about their values, beliefs, and relationships.

Although I had hoped the study would shed some light on how to handle faith questions, George Barna's conclusions reinforced what I already knew: "Parents must take the lead in establishing the centrality of faith experiences and practices for their children. That begins with parents modeling the significance of faith in their lives."

So I delved into Scripture for guidance. The first part of 2 Timothy 3:14 echoed the cry of my heart for my children to continue in what they have been taught—to love and serve the Lord alone. Our responsibility is to point them to Jesus.

The second part of the verse hit hard. Paul urged Timothy to continue in what he had "become convinced of." While we lay a godly foundation, only the Holy Spirit sparks faith and keeps it burning. Human wisdom can't wrap itself around the message of the cross (1 Corinthians 1:18). Our children believe because the Father draws them to his Son (John 6:44). We plant the seeds, and God makes them grow (1 Corinthians 3:6).

**Digging deeper:** How do you handle your children's questions regarding faith? Reflect on Ephesians 3:14-21.

*Statistics are from http://www.barna.org/barna-update/article/ 15-familykids/146-survey-describes-the-ups-and-downs-of-tween-life.

# Searching

Always be prepared to give an answer to everyone who asks you to give the reason for the hope that you have. But do this with gentleness and respect. (1 Peter 3:15)

"What did you do?" a homeschooling friend asked when I mentioned that my daughter had questions about her faith. "I would have had a fit."

Never in my wildest dreams did I imagine that my daughter might have doubts about her faith. *You didn't ground her enough in the faith. It's your fault,* I berated myself. In reality, though, each of us comes to the crossroads where faith becomes personal or not.

First Peter 3:15 provides the foundation for handling questions about faith: gentleness and respect.

**Take the questions seriously.** Aware that how we handled this matter would impact Lisa's openness with us in the future, we engaged her in discussions and sought resources, such as apologetics books, that we could study together with her. We relied on the Holy Spirit to show us what to say during difficult situations (Luke 12:12).

**Step back and refrain from an emotional reaction.** That isn't easy when something as precious and vital as faith is under scrutiny by one's child, but we tried to be gentle and respectful to encourage further communication.

**Discern between questions and challenges.** Like most children, Lisa learns through asking questions and analyzing and processing information. When I realized she was seeking truth, not challenging it, I clung to the promise that those who seek find (Luke 11:9).

**Digging deeper:** Check out *The Case for Christ for Kids*, *The Case for a Creator*, and *A Case for Faith* by Lee Strobel; and *Don't Check Your Brains at the Door: A Book of Christian Evidences (Know What You Believe and Why)* by Josh McDowell and Bob Hostetler.

# An All-Consuming Passion

My soul is consumed with longing for your laws
at all times. (Psalm 119:20)

"These commandments . . . are to be upon your hearts. Impress them on your children" (Deuteronomy 6:6-7). *That's quite a charge, Lord.* I closed my Bible and slid it into the drawer of my nightstand.

Those words stayed with me through the day, and I found myself whispering to the Lord: "It seems like it was easier to impress your words on Lisa's heart when she was younger. How do I encourage a preteen to read her Bible, and follow up without seeming like I'm nagging? You know, Lord she's trying to spread her wings a bit. If I let go of following up on her quiet time, will she have her devotions regularly?"

We had family devotions and started school with prayer and Bible reading. But I didn't want those things to become a substitute for her individual time with the Lord.

Since I knew that developing the habit of Bible reading would stand her in good stead, we started following a reading plan in our separate quiet times. Once a week we discussed what we found meaningful and its application to our lives.

Several months later, peace took hold of my heart with each word of Psalm 119:20: "My soul is consumed with longing for your laws at all times." Jim and I would continue to encourage Lisa in developing the spiritual disciplines of regular Bible reading, prayer, and worship. But only the Lord could cause her heart to be consumed with longing for his Word.

I daily pray Psalm 119:20 over my children, knowing that when God sparks the flame in their hearts, nothing can quench it.

**Digging deeper:** What comfort does Psalm 119:20 offer as you disciple your children?

# Benefits of the Word

I delight in your decrees; I will not neglect
your word. (Psalm 119:16)

"What's going on?" My father leaned toward me in his chair. "I
haven't seen you reading your Bible in weeks."

I stared at the Bangalore skyline through the open balcony
door. As a teenager, myriad other things beckoned me. Silence
hung between us.

"I miss seeing you with your Bible every day. It's your guide
through life. Don't neglect it."

I gave a halfhearted nod.

Several years later, everything for which I had worked academically crumbled when an infection invaded my immune system.

One night, I fought for my life, with the doctor standing by
and my parents praying at my bedside. As I drifted in and out of
consciousness, I recognized that were I to face my Creator, he
wouldn't be impressed with my academic accolades. In the
months of slow recovery, I found the joy of delighting in God's
Word. I realized the truth of Psalm 119:71: "It was good for me to
be afflicted so that I might learn your decrees."

Now, more than twenty years later, I can echo the psalmist, "I
delight in your decrees; I will not neglect your word" because it:

- Purifies me and keeps me from evil (Psalm 119:9,101,
  128,133).
- Guides me (Psalm 119:24,105,133).
- Preserves my life (Psalm 119:25,107,116,154,156,159).
- Strengthens me (Psalm 119:28).
- Gives me freedom (Psalm 119:32,45).
- Gives me understanding (Psalm 119:34,99,100,104,125,
  130,169).
- Brings hope and comfort (Psalm 119:49,50,76,81,114,147).
- Is trustworthy and eternal (Psalm 119:86,89,138,160).

- Gives peace (Psalm 119:165).
- Delivers (Psalm 119:170,173).

**Digging deeper:** What would your life be like without God's Word?

# Temples of the Lord

"Consider now, for the Lord has chosen you
to build a house as a sanctuary. Be strong
and do the work." (1 Chronicles 28:10)

The building of the Lord's temple required 3,600 foremen; a workforce of more than 150,000; cedar, cypress, and juniper from Lebanon; yarns of blue, crimson, and purple; and extravagant amounts of bronze, gold, and silver. Intrigued by this massive undertaking, I studied 1 Kings 5–9 and 2 Chronicles 1–7. I came away strengthened for my homeschooling journey.

God appointed Solomon to build his temple, even though David, his father, desired to do so (1 Chronicles 17:4, 11-14; 28:5-6). It is no accident that we have the children we do—God chose us to parent them. He led us to homeschool—to lay a strong foundation of faith, to build character, and to point them to Jesus. When they come to faith in Jesus, they become temples of the living God (1 Corinthians 3:16-17; 6:19).

God gave David the construction plans in minute detail down to the articles that would be used in the temple, the weight of the gold and silver, and the Levites who would serve (1 Chronicles 28:19). Likewise, God has not left us without guidance in raising our children and homeschooling them. God's Word has everything we need (Psalm 119:105).

The construction of the temple was a huge responsibility, not unlike ours in homeschooling. David assured Solomon, "Be strong and courageous, and do the work. Do not be afraid or discouraged, for the LORD God, my God, is with you. He will not fail you or forsake you" (1 Chronicles 28:20). Those words are as sure today as they were thousands of years ago.

**Digging deeper:** How do today's verses strengthen you to homeschool?

# Solomon's Prayer

When Solomon had finished building the temple of the LORD . . . the LORD said to him: "I have heard the prayer and plea you have made before me." (1 Kings 9:1,3)

Solomon's blessings and prayers at the temple's dedication (1 Kings 8:14-21,23-53,56-61; 2 Chronicles 6:14-21) are as relevant to my homeschooling journey as they were to the children of Israel. They guide my prayers as I homeschool.

- Our homeschooling journey may span more or less than the seven years it took to build the temple. At the end we can echo Solomon's words, "Praise be to the LORD, the God of Israel, who with his hands has fulfilled what he promised" (2 Chronicles 6:4), and "Not one word has failed of all the good promises he gave" (1 Kings 8:56).
- As we release our children to God's plans, Solomon's words again resonate: May God be with them and never leave them nor forsake them. May the Lord turn their hearts to him, to walk in all God's ways and to keep his commands, decrees, and regulations (1 Kings 8:57-60).
- We charge our children to keep their hearts "fully committed to the LORD" (1 Kings 8:61).
- Solomon was realistic about human nature. His words reassure me as I pray for my children. "When they sin against you—for there is no one who does not sin . . . and if they have a change of heart . . . and repent and plead with you . . .

**61**

then . . . hear their prayer and their plea, and uphold their cause. And forgive your people, who have sinned against you" (1 Kings 8:46-50).

We can be assured that as we lift our children to the Lord, our prayers will be heard just as Solomon's were.

**Digging deeper:** Reflect on 2 Chronicles 6:12-42.

[ Gifts We Give Our Children ] **DAY** 58

# "I'm Scared of God"

Come, my children, listen to me; I will teach
you the fear of the LORD. (Psalm 34:11)

"I'm scared of God." Six-year-old Lisa pulled her knees up to her chest as we started our devotions.

I looked at her. "Why would you be scared of God when he loves you?"

"But the Bible tells me to be afraid of God."

I bit back a smile as I remembered our previous night's Bible reading about fearing the Lord. I drew Lisa to me. "The fear of the Lord doesn't mean you have to be scared of God. It means we honor him because he's powerful, mighty, and holy. Yet he loves us."

Psalm 34:11 reminds us to teach our children what the fear of the Lord is and how to live by it.

The concept was huge for Lisa to fathom. How could I help her understand what it means to fear the Lord? As I searched the Scriptures, the answer became clear. "To fear the LORD is to hate evil" (Proverbs 8:13), and "Through the fear of the LORD evil is avoided" (Proverbs 16:6). These verses made it easier for me to explain that when we stay away from things that don't honor God, we are showing him reverence.

*Excellent!*

Lisa began to understand the concept more as we applied that truth to our lives and asked ourselves a few questions: What TV shows, books, and music honored Jesus? How could we treat each other in a God-honoring way? We delved into the Bible to find out what pleased the Lord or not. As we did so, we found guidance for godly living, bringing true wisdom for life (Proverbs 1:7; 9:10; 15:33).

**Digging deeper:** How do you teach your children the fear of the Lord and to live by it?

[ A Faith of Their Own ] **DAY** 59

# "But They Do It"

Keep your father's command and do not forsake your mother's teaching. Bind them always on your heart. . . . When you walk, they will guide you; when you sleep, they will watch over you; when you awake, they will speak to you. (Proverbs 6:20-22)

"But they watch that show, Mama. Why can't I?" Lisa stood with her hands on her hips waiting for my answer.

I sighed. How could I explain to a five-year-old that each family has its own perspectives on such issues?

"You know what, sweetie? If her parents think it's okay for her to watch that show, that's fine. But we won't be watching it."

She tilted her head and then nodded. "Okay, Mommy," and she skipped off to play.

We've revisited the issue in different forms over the years: "Why can't I dress like she does?" "But she listens to that music." "Her mom lets her read those magazines." "She's my age, and *she* wears makeup." Our explanations have taken many forms: We've described what we believe honors God or not. We've read the kid's version of Charles Sheldon's *In His Steps*, encouraged Lisa to ask herself, "What would Jesus do?" and given her a "WWJD" bracelet. And of late we've pointed her to the Mellott Family Values. These values, based on Scripture, serve as our family's written code of conduct. (For example, show compassion and respect, have daily devotional time, and pray before making a decision about what we read, watch, and listen to or even wear.) They are a daily reminder of how to live in a way that honors our Lord. Though we often articulate them, of late, we've asked Lisa to write them down to help her remember them. Proverbs encourages children to heed parental instruction. The Bible also urges parents to make the teaching of God's Word an intrinsic part of daily living (Deuteronomy 11:18-19). Having a tangible code of conduct is our family's way of making God's word a practical part of daily living. It reminds us that our lives are to be influenced by God's word, not by others' choices and actions.

**Digging deeper:** Rearticulate your family values to your children. Reflect on Proverbs 4.

[ Homeschool and You ] **DAY** 60

# Joy in Obedience

"The joy of the Lord is your strength."
(Nehemiah 8:10)

My husband settled into the sofa with a sigh and picked up the newspaper.

"Jim, what do you think of putting Lisa in school?" I had finally voiced what had been lurking in my mind for a few weeks. Instead of the anticipated relief, however, an icy hand gripped my heart. I *knew* at once that I wasn't in line with what God wanted of me.

He put the newspaper down and stared. "Why?"

"Well, it's just . . . I'm tired and overwhelmed."

I was going through the motions of school. A difficult pregnancy, postpartum health issues, homeschooling, and a new baby with erratic sleeping habits were sapping my energy.

Jim moved closer to me on the sofa and took my hands in his. "Lord, strengthen us, especially Anita, to do your will. Show me how I can help her. Oh, and fill her with joy."

*Joy. That's what was missing.* The thought plastered itself across my heart as Jim prayed. Though I was obeying God, I had allowed circumstances to steal my joy in serving him.

The origin of the Hebrew word for *strength* in Nehemiah 8:10 refers to a safe haven—a place where one can rest securely and take shelter. I can find in Jesus a place of refuge and a harbor regardless of my feelings and circumstances. As I dwell in the shadow of his wings, he brings peace. As I abide in him, Jesus allows supernatural joy to bubble up within me no matter what.

**Digging deeper:** What robs you of your joy in obeying God? Reflect on Philippians 3:1 and 4:4.

[ Homeschool Basics] **DAY** 61

# "That's Not Good Enough" *Perfectionism or Excellence?*

Whatever you do, whether in word or deed, do it all
in the name of the Lord Jesus. (Colossians 3:17)

"Nicky, jump farther." Her father stood beside the long jump pit on field day.

After the kids in the line finished their turn, Nicky jumped again. Her father leaned forward, fists clenched. "That's not good enough. You've *got* to try harder."

She rose in one fluid motion. "I'm not listening to you." Hands over her ears, she sashayed off the pit.

*What message do I send my children?* I wondered.

Mediocrity isn't an option for Christians. It's easy, though, to mistake excellence for perfectionism. Excellence is doing one's best, realizing that the end result may not be perfect. Perfectionism is expecting flawlessness.

I often struggle with avoiding perfectionism while encouraging my children to excellence. The following checklist keeps me in line:

- Did my children do their best? If so, that's reward enough.
- Do I dwell on mistakes rather than celebrate a job well done?
- Do I focus on every minute detail being perfect?
- Is there a point at which I can let go?
- Do I feel pressure, or do I put my children under pressure to win all the time?

The Bible offers the perfect antidote for perfectionism in Colossians 3:17. The reminder to do everything in the name of the Lord Jesus takes the focus off us—our motives and what we want the results to be. Often wanting to feel good about ourselves, being concerned about how others perceive us, and fearing failure drives perfectionism. Working at a task to give the Lord glory puts things into the right perspective.

**Digging deeper:** How do you encourage excellence in school? Reflect on Ecclesiastes 9:10.

[ Homeschool Basics ] **DAY** 62

# "What's Wrong with Being Average?"

"To one he gave five bags of gold, to another two bags, and to another one bag, each according to his ability. Then he went on his journey." (Matthew 25:15)

"What's wrong with being average, Mommy?" Lisa, then eight years old, cupped her face in her hands as she looked at me across the desk.

"Nothing, as long as that's how God made you." I slid her math work sheets across the desk. "But in this case," I pointed to the careless mistakes, "you're smart. You need to live up to the potential God has given you. It takes hard work to get there."

She turned and looked out the window. I reached for the Bible and found the parable of the talents.

I had always wondered why the master was so annoyed with the servant who buried the money. As I studied verse 15 and the meaning of the word *ability*, two things became clear: (1) God blesses each of us with inherent abilities, and (2) each individual is responsible for developing those abilities.

The master knew each servant's ability, and he expected them to live up to that potential. The "lazy, wicked" servant didn't put any effort into getting a return on the money. In fact, he did "less than the least" (v. 26, MSG), resulting in the master's outrage.

As stewards, we are to develop the abilities with which God has blessed us, use them for his glory, and encourage our children to do the same. If not, we are unworthy of God's trust. "It is required that those who have been given a trust must prove faithful" (1 Corinthians 4:2).

**Digging deeper:** Reflect on Matthew 25:14-30.

[ Homeschool Basics ] **DAY** 63

# "Well Done, Good and Faithful Servant!"

"'Well done, good and faithful servant! You have been faithful with a few things; I will put you in charge of many things. Come and share your master's happiness!'" (Matthew 25:21)

What a delight to hear these words at the end of our journey!

So how can we, as parents, encourage our children to develop the talents God has given them?

*Excellent check list*

- Pray. "My husband and I ask God to show us our children's talents and what we can do to encourage them," a home-schooling mom shared. Their intentionality in encouraging their children's talents has inspired me.
- Be intentional about providing opportunities to pursue those interests—from instruction to fun activities, field trips, or even internships or apprenticeships.
- Keep in mind the ages of your children and what they are capable of doing. The key is to nurture and develop a love for their interests.
- Involve them. Talk to them about their likes and interests and how God can use them, especially as they grow older.
- Teach them the value of being good stewards of the special abilities with which God has blessed them.
- As they grow older, encourage them to pray about ways to use their talents to further God's kingdom.
- Examine motives beginning with yourself. Are your children involved in activities that interest them or you? To what end are you encouraging the pursuit and development of their talents? Is bringing glory to God the main reason your children want to pursue a particular area of interest?

**Digging deeper:** How do you encourage your children's interests?

[ Homeschool Basics ] **DAY** 64

# Love, No Matter What

Love never fails. (1 Corinthians 13:8)

"Our girls' performance isn't an indicator of our love for them or their worth." Susie, a friend and homeschooling mom, shared her family's experience in encouraging their children's interests.

Both girls excelled in their talents. Thirteen-year-old Ann competed in piano competitions for several years, and ten-year-old Christie competed successfully in gymnastics.

"We've always prayed that God would reveal their talents and give them opportunities to pursue them. But we pray about our motives. Are they pursuing their talents to give God the glory?"

Recently Ann didn't win Outstanding Performer in a piano competition and missed going to the state level—an opportunity that had been hers for a few years. Failing to take the top spot gave her the chance to examine her motives. She decided to continue piano lessons because God was calling her to do so.

In contrast, Christie, a gifted competitive gymnast, decided she didn't want to pursue the sport anymore. "My medals don't matter," she told her parents. Susie was thrilled that her younger daughter "had the discernment to step back."

"Our girls know that it doesn't matter if they don't win. Christie missed first place by .25 in a meet, but we cheered hard for her. Their diligence in preparing and their perseverance build character. We focus on what it takes to get there, not the winning. Their character will last long after the event is won.

"We encourage them to do their best. But our love isn't based on how they do. That gives them the freedom to take their interests as far as they want to."

Susie underscored an important value—love never fails. Our love for our children exists and is displayed no matter what, just like Christ's love for us.

**Digging deeper:** How is unconditional love displayed in your homeschool?

# Speak Encouragement Today

Encourage one another daily, as long
as it is called "Today." (Hebrews 3:13)

My father seldom praised me. He believed it was better to point
out what I didn't do right. "It's the only way you'll grow and
improve," he often commented. "If I don't tell you, then who
will?"

I worked hard to prove myself. Whenever I achieved something, his reaction was, "You performed as expected." Nothing
changed, not even when I got the first rank in the state for my
postgraduate degree in journalism. "I didn't expect any less,"
was all he said.

When my husband and I moved to the United States years
later, I worked as a writer/editor for Habitat for Humanity International. I sent my parents copies of my articles and the publica-
tions for which I was responsible. My father acknowledged each
of them with "Thanks."

One morning four years later, tears blurred my eyes as I read
and reread my father's e-mail: "Your magazines are terrific!" I
printed out that message and kept it in my Bible. I read it often,
my fingers tracing his words. It became even more precious
when he passed away two days later.

In the following months, many of his friends shared, "Your
Dad was so proud of you and what you do. He loved you a lot."

*Why didn't he ever tell me himself? Why did he wait so long?* I wondered. Thirty-three years had passed as I waited for a word of
affirmation from him. That made me determined to speak
encouragement daily over my children.

"Lord, open my eyes for ways to encourage my children, to celebrate their potential while I have the chance" is my prayer each day.

**Digging deeper:** Celebrate your children today. Reflect on Proverbs 15:23 and 16:24.

# Disapproval's Sting

My thoughts trouble me and I am distraught.
(Psalm 55:2)

"I don't understand this 'homeschooling' thing you're doing, Anita. When are you going to put that poor child in school?" Aunty Maria, who was like a second mother to me, smiled and patted my hand. I was crushed.

I was no stranger to disapproval about homeschooling. It stung more from close friends in India, where homeschooling was an unknown and education had high value.

Disapproval hurts, whether a person expresses it implicitly or explicitly. The more significant that person is in our lives, the deeper the hurt. "If an enemy were insulting me, I could endure it. . . . But it is you . . . my companion, my close friend" (Psalm 55:12-13).

The root of the hurt often lies in our subconscious desire to be liked and to have others respect and affirm what we do. Unfortunately, that sets in motion a vicious circle of questions that lead to doubt. Doubts prey on our minds, making us vulnerable to straying from the path to which God has led us.

Prayerfully consider these questions:

- Why does disapproval cause such emotional turmoil?
- Are we looking for validation or praise from others?
- Are we insecure about our decision to homeschool or about our homeschool program?

*If God has called you to his then it doesn't matter what others think!*

As we seek the Lord, the Spirit will expose the motives of our heart (1 Corinthians 4:5).

Psalm 55 reveals David's agony at being hurt by a close friend. The outpouring of his heart mirrors my feelings when I encounter disapproval from those close to me. But more than that, this psalm brings peace—God hears my distress and saves me (vv. 16-17). God understands my turmoil and will sustain me as I cast my cares on him (v. 22).

**Digging deeper:** How do you handle disapproval from friends and family about homeschooling? Reflect on Psalm 55.

[ Homeschool and You ] **DAY** 67

# The Approval That Matters the Most

"Your journey has the LORD's approval."
(Judges 18:6)

"So, are you *still* homeschooling?" Aunty Reena, a close friend and former school principal, put her arm around me and led me into her condo.

My joy at being reunited with family and friends in India evaporated. The tacit suggestion that I was spoiling my child's future by homeschooling drained me.

"Um, yes, Aunty." I looked away. *How do I give her a firm but polite answer without hurting her feelings?* I wondered, aware of my culture's high standards of respect for elders.

"How does it help *her*?" Her tone grew curious as she nodded toward eight-year-old Lisa.

That night, after I put Lisa to bed, I stood on the balcony of my parents' condo. Aunty's words, "How does it help *her*?" played over and over in my mind.

"Lord, help me," I prayed. I rested my hands on the cool, rough surface of the balcony wall and gazed at Bangalore's nightscape. The lights sparkled against the dark velvet sky, relaxing me a bit.

A gentle whisper within probed: *Why do you homeschool?* I looked up and smiled. "Because you led us to, Lord," I whispered.

Jim and I had agreed that homeschooling was God's will for our family. God knew best. A sense of peace, like a blanket, wrapped itself around me. I snuggled into it and smiled.

**Digging deeper:** Have you found a place of rest in God's leading to homeschool? Reflect on Psalm 62:1-8.

[ Homeschool Foundations ] **DAY** 68

# Prayer
## key to Dealing with Disapproval—Part 1

Hear my prayer, Lord; let my cry for help come to you.
Do not hide your face from me when I am in distress.
Turn your ear to me; when I call, answer me quickly.
(Psalm 102:1-2)

A few weeks after my trip to India, I relaxed in my sunroom with Julie, a friend and homeschooling mom of three. We exchanged stories about encountering disapproval.

"My parents think my kids should be in school. I deal with disapproval from them all the time," Julie shared.

"So how do you handle it?" I asked.

"Anita, I pray." Her eyes brightened. "It's the key to dealing with disapproval."

She was right.

**Pray for discernment while talking to those who question homeschooling.** Not every question is motivated by disapproval.

Ask God for help to distinguish between curiosity and criticism. The former deserves a thoughtful response.

**Pray for discretion.** When questions express disapproval, consider whether an answer is necessary. Silence speaks louder than words. Jesus was silent in the face of his accusers (Acts 8:32). "I will watch my ways and keep my tongue from sin; I will put a muzzle on my mouth" (Psalm 39:1).

**Pray for self-control.** Sometimes a response may be required. God can give us restraint and gentleness in the face of disapproval. Speaking in the heat of the moment has no benefit. In Proverbs 17:27, using words with restraint and being even-tempered are signs of understanding and wisdom, which are only God-given.

**Digging deeper:** Reflect on Psalm 102:1-17 and Matthew 26:57-67.

[ Homeschool Foundations ] **DAY** 69

# Prayer
## key to Dealing with Disapproval—Part 2

"Look to the LORD and his strength; seek his face always."
(1 Chronicles 16:11)

First Chronicles 16:11 is a powerful balm when we face disapproval on the path to which God has led us. To "seek his face," or his presence, can heal the hurts of disapproval and strengthen us to "keep his way" (Psalm 37:34).

**Pray for forgiveness.** Forgiving in the face of hurt can be difficult. But hurt that is not dealt with can lead to bitterness. Jesus, who forgives us, will help us to do the same with others no matter how deep the hurt. "Bear with each other and forgive one another if any of you has a grievance against someone. Forgive as the Lord forgave you" (Colossians 3:13).

**Pray for healing.** Often, disapproval leaves bruised feelings and emotions in its wake. Though we may have forgiven, the ache remains. Jesus is no stranger to grief and hurt. He soothes and heals battered emotions. "He heals the brokenhearted and binds up their wounds" (Psalm 147:3).

**Pray for strength and grace to stay the path despite what others say.** Scripture promises that God "will keep in perfect peace" those with a steadfast mind who trust in the Lord (Isaiah 26:3).

**Pray for eternity's perspective.** What matters in the end? Paul's question and conclusion are worth keeping in mind: "Am I now trying to win the approval . . . of God? Or am I trying to please people? If I were still trying to please people, I would not be a servant of Christ" (Galatians 1:10).

**Digging deeper:** How has prayer helped you in the face of disapproval? Reflect on 1 Thessalonians 5:13-15.

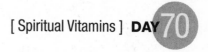

[ Spiritual Vitamins ] **DAY** 70

# Tiny Seeds

Get rid of all bitterness, rage and anger, brawling and slander, along with every form of malice. (Ephesians 4:31)

"Mommy, Mommy." I hurried at the urgency in nine-year-old Lisa's voice. We almost collided as she ran down the stairs.

"I found the back of my earring!"

"Where is it?"

She tilted her head upward and moved closer to me.

"There."

"Here?" I looked where she was pointing—the back of her earlobe—and my heart sank. I struggled against the nausea. *What a horrible mother I am. I should have looked harder three months ago.*

I gently pressed her swollen ear lobe. She winced. I felt the hard rim of the earring back under the red, infected skin. "I'm afraid I'll have to take you to the doctor, sweetie. I can't take this out by myself."

A few hours later, the doctor numbed the area and dug around.

*Help me not to be sick, Lord,* I prayed as I held Lisa's hand.

"Voilà!" The pediatrician turned to me and held up the offender in her tweezers.

How tiny it was.

Lisa struggled to sit up and moaned. The doctor turned just in time to catch her as she fainted. It took several days and a round of antibiotics before Lisa was back to normal.

Ephesians 4:31 took on deeper meaning during that time. Often, huge, out-of-control issues start from a tiny seed. Misunderstandings lead to conflicts, bitterness to unforgiveness, unhealthy habits to addictions, pride to self-righteousness, and the surreptitious look to adultery. "Lord," I prayed, "uproot the tiny seeds of evil and selfishness in me before they spiral out of control."

**Digging deeper:** What tiny seed of evil, bitterness, or discontent is festering inside you? Reflect on Genesis 4:1-16.

[ Homeschool and You ] **DAY** 71

# "Where Did She Hear *That?*"

"Holy Father, protect them by the power of your name, the name you gave me." (John 17:11)

"Mommy, what's a pimp?"

I spun around. "Where did you hear that word?" I asked, staring at eight-year-old Lisa.

"At co-op."

*Co-op? We're homeschoolers. Who used that word?*

That incident emphasized that the world intrudes on our homeschool lives, whether through friends, the media, or displays in stores. I can't keep my children isolated to prevent these influences, but I can teach them what's right and wrong from God's Word, and encourage them to choose righteousness and purity.

Before Jesus was crucified, he prayed for his disciples and all who would believe in him. That prayer reassures me, and guides my prayers for my children.

**"My prayer is not that you take them out of the world but that you protect them from the evil one"** (John 17:15). My responsibility is to prepare my children for life—to give them the tools to combat the influences of the world. I pray for wisdom and discernment for them, that they would be salt and light rather than be influenced, and that God would protect their hearts.

**"Protect them by the power of your name"** (John 17:11). In Hebrew tradition, names were more than labels by which to call people. Names embodied and represented the person. When Jesus asked the Father to protect his disciples by the power of his name, he was calling on everything God is to guard and keep them. The name that is above every other name is the name that protects our children. When we call on the name of Jesus, we are tapping into a mighty storehouse of supernatural power and authority.

**Digging deeper:** How does John 17 help you in praying for wisdom and discernment for your children?

[ A Faith of Their Own ] **DAY** 72

# Blurry Moral Lines

Noah was a righteous man, blameless among
the people of his time, and he walked faithfully
with God. (Genesis 6:9)

"Mom."

I looked up at the seriousness of Lisa's tone. She explained that a friend at Bible study had requested prayer for a classmate who was pregnant.

"Mom, she's only twelve, like me!" Her voice rose.

It brought home the realities of the world in which we live—a world of blurry moral lines. It reminded me of the days of Noah, where wickedness was rampant and "every inclination . . . of the human heart was only evil all the time" (Genesis 6:5). Yet Noah found favor with God (v. 8).

Jesus warns that wickedness will increase and the love of most will grow cold (Matthew 24:12). How do we equip our children to walk with God, like Noah did?

We can:

- Be unashamed about the Bible being our compass and help our children see its relevance in this age. "Your word is a lamp for my feet, a light on my path" (Psalm 119:105).
- Engage our children about issues—explain what we believe to be right and wrong from a biblical perspective, and why. "Direct my footsteps according to your word" (Psalm 119:133).
- Cultivate an open relationship so our children can ask us questions without feeling judged. "Take them by the hand and lead them in the way of the Master" (Ephesians 6:4, MSG).
- Above all, point children to the cross and its message of grace. We are ambassadors of hope because of God's love. "But God demonstrates his own love for us in this: While we were still sinners, Christ died for us" (Roman 5:8). We can be gentle and humble in our witness because of God's grace.

**Digging deeper:** How do you prepare your children to face the world and its influences? Reflect on Genesis 6.

# Open Communication

Take note of this: Everyone should be quick to listen,
slow to speak and slow to become angry. (James 1:19)

"Mom." Lisa interrupted our Latin review. "That prayer request I heard at Bible study is really bothering me," she confided almost a week later.

I put the flash cards aside. "Why?"

"Well, she's so young to have a baby."

We spent most of the morning discussing purity and temptation.

Though I've often prayed that I would be approachable, someone to whom my kids can come with *anything*, it isn't easy to develop and maintain open communication.

James 1:19 offers some valuable advice in this regard:

- **Listen.** Rather than following my first instinct to "fix it" and tell my preteen what to do, I should be "quick to listen." When I listen, I communicate my interest in what she has to say. Listening lays the foundation for her being open when I do offer advice.
- **Affirm.** Ways to affirm our children abound—not only for doing the right thing or achieving something, but for effort and character. My being "slow to speak" critical or harsh words goes a long way in affirming my children.
- **Confess and repent.** Sometimes I misunderstand or jump to conclusions. I'm learning to be quick to admit I was wrong and ask forgiveness of the Lord and of my daughter. I'm trying to be "slow to become angry" or indignant.
- **Love unconditionally.** It's vital to communicate acceptance at every stage of parenting. Accepting our children for who they are rather than who we would like them to be is crucial in developing self-esteem.

**Digging deeper:** What do you do to encourage your children to come to you about anything? Reflect on 1 Peter 1:13-15.

# Discernment

"Give your servant a discerning heart to govern your people and to distinguish between right and wrong." (1 Kings 3:9)

"Anita, you know how protective I was." My homeschooling friend Laura leaned toward me.

I nodded. I was used to Laura hovering over her four kids.

She continued, "Since we moved to Atlanta, Kevin and I have been sensing God leading me to let go a bit. And God's been helping me. It's all about trust."

Laura went on to describe a visit with a new friend and her family. While Laura and her friend visited, the kids went into the yard to play. After a while, her friend's son started talking about movies he liked and invited them to his room to watch a few. Laura's thirteen-year-old, Ethan, was uncomfortable with some of the movie choices.

"Anita, I didn't know what was going on. But Ethan not only told the boy they couldn't watch the movie, he told his siblings not to go in either." Her eyes danced. "I was so proud of my son."

She leaned across the restaurant table. "God showed me something that day. Kevin and I teach and train our kids. We raise them according to the Scriptures. But then we have to trust God and let them go. We have to give them the opportunity to prove to us that we can trust them."

When God asked Solomon what he wanted, Solomon requested a "discerning heart . . . to distinguish between right and wrong." That's what I pray for my children each day.

Laura's words challenged me. They also encouraged me that God empowers his people—regardless of age—to live as he calls us to.

**Digging deeper:** How have your children displayed discernment and trustworthiness? Reflect on Proverbs 3:21-26.

# Watch Your Diet

Above all else, guard your heart, for everything
you do flows from it. (Proverbs 4:23)

I held my breath as the nurse drew blood. The seconds ticked
away while we waited for the results to show up on the tiny
monitor. My heart plunged. I had gestational diabetes.

For the rest of the pregnancy, I recorded my sugar levels six
times a day so my doctor could review them every week.

Exercise wasn't an option because of my high-risk pregnancy.
So I watched my diet. I counted carbs, weighed every ounce of
food that went on my plate, and said no to sugar.

The hard work paid off. Though my sugar levels were high, I
didn't need insulin.

*What would my life be like if I guarded my heart the way I watch my
diet?* I wondered as I read Proverbs 4:23.

The underlying sense of the verse goes beyond being careful. It
means being vigilant 24/7 about what goes into our hearts. The
heart is more than an organ that keeps us alive. From a biblical
perspective, it's the center of one's thoughts, emotions, intellect,
choices, and decisions. It is a wellspring of life influencing how
we live.

Jesus said, "A tree is recognized by its fruit. . . . The mouth
speaks what the heart is full of. The good man brings good things
out of the good stored up in him, and an evil man brings evil
things out of the evil stored up in him" (Matthew 12:33-35).

Our commitment to guarding our hearts will encourage our
children to do so as well. Our actions speak louder than words.

**Digging deeper:** How do you guard your heart and encourage
your children to do so? Reflect on Matthew 7:16-20, 12:33.

# An Anchor through the Storms

When you pass through the waters, I will be with you;
and when you pass through the rivers, they will not
sweep over you. (Isaiah 43:2)

Life brings good and bad. For homeschoolers, situations in our personal lives ripple through school.

As we've homeschooled through some of life's storms—illness, death, job loss, relocation—some truths have anchored us:

**God is sovereign. Nothing surprises him.** Within weeks of discovering I was pregnant after nine years, I lay on a gurney. My OB/GYN pointed to a waterfall-like image on the ultrasound screen. "You're hemorrhaging across the placenta and cervix. All I can do is put you on bed rest."

The Psalms became my refuge during an uncertain time. The raw outpouring of David's heart mirrored mine. The strong strand of faith in his writing undergirded me.

"All the days ordained for me were written in your book before one of them came to be" (Psalm 139:16). God knew we would homeschool through this uncertain time. He held our baby in his hands. I could rest in that assurance.

**God protects us.** "When you pass through the waters, I will be with you; and when you pass through the rivers, they will not sweep over you" (Isaiah 43:2). When, after twelve weeks, the ultrasound revealed a heartbeat, my doctor was "cautiously optimistic." But each week brought new concerns for us, with weekly visits to the OB/GYN or perinatologist.

Jesus let neither the rivers overwhelm us nor the fire scorch us.

**God is merciful.** For every day in the valley, God's mercies were new—whether prayer via a phone call, an encouraging e-mail, or someone bringing a meal. His faithfulness was great (Lamentations 3:22-23).

No matter how fierce the storm in your life, Jesus will never let you face it alone.

**Digging deeper:** In what way do challenges in your personal life affect school? Reflect on Isaiah 43:1-2.

[ Homeschool Basics ] **DAY** 77

# Homeschooling through the Storms

... he who made a way through the sea, a path through the mighty waters. (Isaiah 43:16)

It's hard to homeschool through difficulties, especially when the primary home educator is hit. But the one who led us to this path will make a way "through the mighty waters" (Isaiah 43:16).

I've learned some lessons over the years:

- **Be realistic.** During my second pregnancy, my bed rest went from a few weeks to almost the whole pregnancy. I wondered how we'd cope with school and attend co-op and activities. When days developed into weeks where, wracked with nausea and pain, I could barely pull myself up in bed, I had to be realistic about school.
- **Be flexible.** I let some things go—like working a grade level ahead in math and trying to finish the curriculum in 180 days; we could catch up during the summer. Whenever a bout of energy hit me, nine-year-old Lisa jumped into my bed with math and grammar. My mother and husband helped with other subjects.
- **Accept help.** Though we had relocated to Atlanta only a year prior, the church and the homeschooling community encompassed us with love. They carried our burdens (Galatians 6:2), whether it was driving me to doctor's appointments, bringing meals, or taking my daughter to co-op and field trips.

- **Embrace life lessons.** Lisa's education didn't suffer, as the standardized testing revealed. Beyond that, she experienced God's faithfulness through the crucible of life. "God gave me a baby sister when I'd been praying all my life for one, Mommy. Then God let you and her live even though the doctors didn't think so," she shared several months later. What a life lesson—that the sun still peeks through the clouds and there's a rainbow after the storm.

*Beautiful*

**Digging deeper:** What lessons has your family learned through life's crucibles? Reflect on Psalm 23.

# When Your Child Is Sick

My soul, find rest in God; my hope comes from him.
. . . He is my fortress, I will not be shaken. (Psalm 62:5-6)

*From Barbara King, whose fourteen-year-old daughter has a rare form of cystic fibrosis:*

We decided to homeschool Olivia after her first liver transplant at age four. Little did I know the challenges it would bring.

Often, she is too sick to finish a day's schoolwork. I'm learning to balance my mom's heart and school.

*Lovely*

- **Be realistic.** Your children may not be able to learn the "normal" way. Give them achievable goals so they can feel satisfied.
- **Shape your schooling to fit your child.** Olivia is bright, but she's still behind in some subjects because of her illness. I have to remember that each situation is unique and not compare us with other homeschoolers.
- **Concentrate on one subject.** It's easier for Olivia to work through a full year's work in one subject at a time.
- **Listen to the Holy Spirit and press on.** I don't walk in Olivia's shoes, but I see how she feels. I want to wrap her in

my arms and let school go. She, on the other hand, thinks I'm pushing her. When I listen to the Holy Spirit, the balance becomes clear.

- **Time with your child is a gift.** My friend's thirteen-year-old daughter needed a liver transplant. One day she was struggling with school. The next day she was gone. My friend said, "Time is a special gift. Sometimes schoolwork has to be on the back burner. Allow yourself to do that." So some days we just "be" with each other.

It's not easy being Olivia's mom or teacher, but I wouldn't have it any other way. I rely on the Lord every moment—"my hope comes from him. . . . I will not be shaken."

**Digging deeper:** What does Psalm 62:5-6 mean to you as you homeschool?

[ And a Child Will Lead Them ] **DAY** 79

# A Happy Heart

A happy heart makes the face cheerful.
(Proverbs 15:13)

Isaac's eyes sparkled. "Mom, we have to be there early. I want to try every instrument." For the first time in my friend's son's eleven years, Isaac was able to audition for something at school.

When they reached the school, his eyes grew wide at the array of instruments. He grabbed a flute and blew into the mouthpiece as the teacher explained how to position his lips and how to place his fingers.

"I can't do that." He lifted his hands, revealing four fingers on each hand.

"I'm sorry." Red tinged her cheeks. "I didn't know."

"That's okay." Isaac grinned and skipped from room to room. He couldn't blow into the mouthpieces of some instruments, such as the trumpet, and other instruments he couldn't hold because of his clubbed arm.

The last option was the clarinet. His eyes danced at its sound as he blew into the mouthpiece. The teacher pointed out the difficulty of playing it with eight fingers and a shorter left arm. Undaunted, Isaac consulted the band director, who brought out another instrument from the back of the room.

At the sight of the euphonium—a small tubalike instrument with a large mouthpiece, Isaac grinned. His grin grew even wider when he realized the instrument could rest on his lap and had only three keys.

According to his mother, Isaac "finds joy in everything." Nothing undermined his delight in participating in the auditions. Isaac's "happy heart," drives his positive outlook on life—thirty-nine surgeries for heart and spinal cord conditions and a clubbed hand haven't diminished his zest for life and his joie de vivre.

**Digging deeper:** How can you have joy despite adversity? Reflect on Proverbs 15:15,30.

[ Spiritual Vitamins ] **DAY** 80

# All Things Work for Good

We know that in all things God works for the good of those who love him, who have been called according to his purpose. (Romans 8:28)

"Anita, we weren't sure how we'd come out of our situation. But now I can look back and see how God provided." Angie's voice bubbled with joy. I pictured my homeschool friend's eyes shining on the other side of the phone.

In early 2008, Brian, her husband, lost his job. In the following months, the three houses in which he and his business partner invested lay empty in a market that was spiraling downward.

"But God was so good. Brian lost his job early in the housing crisis. After seven months, he got another job. It didn't pay as much, but at least he got a job before the market was flooded with more unemployed people."

She went on recounting God's faithfulness. "Our marriage survived our financial crisis, unlike our business partner's. And we didn't lose our own house."

When Angie reconnected with a former colleague, he offered her a job despite her not having worked for twelve years. "I work from home. My hours are flexible. I still homeschool and can take care of my parents."

She continued counting her blessings. "When I went for my first staff meeting, the first thing everyone did was take prayer requests! All my colleagues are believers. God put me in a perfect place."

During Brian's unemployment, they fasted and prayed for twenty days. "Our kids joined us. They didn't fast from food, but from things they thought they couldn't live without. The best thing is that they experienced God's goodness and faithfulness and came out stronger for it."

**Digging deeper:** How has God brought your family through the valleys of life?

[ Gifts We Give Our Children ] **DAY** 81

# Contentment

Godliness with contentment is great gain.
(1 Timothy 6:6)

"Mom! You should see their house. It's huge. Their basement is full of fun stuff. And you should see her room. . . ." Over the last few weeks, eleven-year-old Lisa couldn't stop talking about all that her friend had when she returned from visits. This time something inside me snapped. My chair toppled over as I stood up.

"That's it. Come here." Her eyes widened as I grabbed her hand.

"Look." I gestured to our family room and pulled her through each room of the house. "What do you see?"

"Stuff?"

"Not just 'stuff.' It's God's blessings. God gave Daddy a good job, and he works hard. How would you like to live like the kids on the streets of India? Why can't you see what God's given us and be grateful?"

"I–I'm s–sorry, Mom." Tears streaked her face.

I dropped her hand and stormed off. Later, after I apologized, I began to think more clearly. *How easy it is to focus on what we don't have. How can we teach contentment? And what exactly is contentment?*

Contentment is being satisfied no matter what. The root of the Greek word used in 1 Timothy 6:6 conveys the sense of being satisfied with what we have, even if it is meager.

Contentment is linked to godliness, or our attitude toward and faith in God. The more we look to Jesus as the one who provides all we need, the greater our contentment.

Discontent stems from envy, greed, and covetousness. Jesus warns us to be on our guard against all kinds of greed. Our lives are not measured by our possessions. Rather, they are measured by the richness of our relationship with God (Luke 12:15,21).

**Digging deeper:** Reflect on Luke 12:13-34.

*really good devotional.*

# Learning Contentment

I know what it is to be in need, and I know what it is
to have plenty. I have learned the secret of being content
in any and every situation, whether well fed or hungry,
whether living in plenty or in want. (Philippians 4:12)

Paul's words, "I have learned the secret of being content in any and every situation" gave me hope. Contentment is learned—the result of our gratitude, trust, and reliance on the Lord.

**Be thankful.** God blesses us with everything—from skills, talents, and intelligence to the ability to work (Deuteronomy 8:18). We didn't bring anything into the world, and we won't take anything when we leave (1 Timothy 6:7). We can't help but fall before God in gratitude when we realize that apart from the Lord we "have no good thing," and that God has assigned us our "portion and cup" and has made our lot secure (Psalm 16:2,5).

**Trust.** "My God will meet all your needs according to the riches of his glory in Christ Jesus" (Philippians 4:19). God knows what we need and will take care of us. When this truth seeps into our hearts, we can "quiet" the anxiety of our souls and rest "like a weaned child with its mother" (Psalm 131:2).

**Delight in the Lord.** Psalm 37:4 calls us to delight in the Lord. When God is our source, nothing else matters. That's the reason Paul could say, "Whatever were gains to me I now consider a loss because of the surpassing worth of knowing Christ Jesus my Lord.... I consider them garbage, that I may gain Christ" (Philippians 3:7-8).

**Digging deeper:** How does Philippians 4:12 enhance your understanding of contentment and equip you to teach your children contentment?

# I Give You Jesus

Then Peter said, "Silver or gold I do not have,
but what I do have I give you. In the name of
Jesus Christ of Nazareth, walk." (Acts 3:6)

*Through the eyes of the beggar:*
    I lean against the wall, my legs sprawled out in front of me,
loose and awkward. Lame from birth, I have no hope of a life
other than begging. I'm useless according to the whispers that
I've overheard. At least at the temple gates I can snag the occa-
sional coin from a rich Pharisee. As the crowds approach for the
afternoon prayers, I sense eyes on me.
    "Look at me!" The strong voice is mesmerizing. My pulse
quickens. I cup my palms together and hold them out.
    "Silver or gold I do not have." Confusion grips me. *No money?*
    "But what I do have I give you." My breath grows erratic.
*What is he offering?*
    "In the name of Jesus Christ of Nazareth. . ." *Jesus? The prophet
who was crucified?*
    "Rise up and walk." *Walk? I've never walked in my whole life.
These men are crazy. Help!* Desperate, I look around. A strong arm
yanks me up. As the blood rushes to my head, I fall forward. A
hand steadies me. My shaky ankles grow firm. I am standing! I
gaze at my legs holding me up. I take a tentative step, and
another—I'm walking! Flinging my crutches away, I leap and
dance, praising God.
    Peter and John gave me something beyond my expectations—
life! But more than that, they gave me hope in the name of Jesus.
He's a gift worth more than anything this world can ever offer.

**Digging deeper:** What gift can you give your children this week?
Reflect on Matthew 13:44-46.

*a great picture of our release from sin!*

# Hurrying Off

So they hurried off and found Mary and Joseph, and
the baby, who was lying in the manger. (Luke 2:16)

Would I get everything done in time for Christmas? I stared at
my to-do list, feeling as if Christmas had sneaked up on me after
a busy Thanksgiving. Would I have the time to bake, entertain,
and finish up the Christmas cards and the semester's schoolwork? The thoughts dampened my joy at Christmas.

Over the next few days, in keeping with my Advent tradition, I read Matthew's and Luke's accounts of Jesus' birth. The
words "They hurried off and found Mary and Joseph, and the
baby, who was lying in the manger" (Luke 2:16) kept coming
back to me.

I imagined the shepherds, terrified at first, as a blinding light
lit up the dark night sky. Then, spellbound, they listened to the
exquisite harmony of the angelic chorus, "Glory to God in the
highest." As the last notes faded, I pictured the shepherds staring
at each other, eyes wide. The flocks bleated and scattered, as the
shepherds, almost falling over themselves, hurried off—to tackle
their Christmas to-do lists—to shop, bake, and decorate.

No! They hurried off to see the baby whose birth the angels
had announced. In fact, that baby—Jesus—was the sole focus of
every participant in that Christmas account.

As that truth began to permeate my heart in the following
days, the chains of being busy with preparations for the season
began to snap and fall away. I bowed in prayer. "Lord, thank you
for reminding me that all that matters is you. Forgive me for getting sidetracked by Christmas preparations. Help me hurry off to
you this season and always."

**Digging deeper:** What is your focus during Christmas?

*Run to Jesus!*

# The Season's Reason

On coming to the house, they saw the child with his
mother Mary, and they bowed down and worshiped him.
Then they opened their treasures and presented him
with gifts of gold, frankincense, and myrrh. (Matthew 2:11)

Just as the wise men's one purpose in today's verse was to find
the Christ child and worship him, Jim and I looked for ways to
keep our Christmas celebrations more worshipful.

**Simplify.** Rather than baking several kinds of cookies, I baked
two family favorites. Instead of wrestling with the crowds in the
mall and taking a chance on items being in the stores, I shopped
online.

Rather than having large parties, we entertained a few families
at a time. We hosted get-togethers after Christmas, reminding us
that celebrating our Savior isn't restricted to only one day.

**Practice meaningful traditions.** Our Advent traditions of
lighting candles and opening the calendars took on deeper meaning as Bible readings in *A Family Celebration of Advent: Keeping the
Savior in the Season* (Thomas Nelson: 2008) grounded us. Our girls
loved the family activities and the stories behind the legends and
celebrations of Christmas. When the girls blew out the candles,
we discussed ways in which we, through sin, extinguish Jesus'
light in our lives.

As we decorated, we reflected on the ornaments that represented fun memories and God's faithfulness.

**Give.** For my parents, Christmas was rarely a family-only celebration. Drawing from that, we opened our home to those who
were alone over the holidays.

Also, rather than wish lists, we asked our kids to think of ways
in which they could give to others.

As we kept Jesus at the center of our family and celebrations,
our joy that Christmas spilled into the new year.

**Digging deeper:** What does your family do to keep celebrations
meaningful?

# Homeschooling's Creativity

In the beginning God created the heavens and the earth. . . . And the Spirit of God was hovering over the waters. (Genesis 1:1-2)

"Where are the conjugations and declensions, Lisa?" I asked as I reviewed my twelve-year-old's Latin work.

"I didn't do them."

"I thought you said you did Latin." I glanced at the clock. "What were you doing for an hour?"

"Here are my maps." She handed me two maps of the United States—one that she had copied and the other from memory.

"So you did geography before you completed Latin. I'll . . ."

"Yeah, I'll go back to Latin now and then."

"Why can't you finish one subject and then move on to the next?"

"It's boring."

"Boring? How are you going to manage at high school or college?" She looked away.

I stared at her wondering, *Should we do things her way or mine? What about the discipline of working through one subject at a time?*

We experimented in the following weeks. I gave her a time limit to complete all schoolwork. She agreed to check off completed tasks in each subject to help her know what work was remaining. Within a month we had a rhythm that worked for both of us. After a few months, I asked her to tackle two tasks in a subject rather than one before moving to another subject. By the end of the semester, she was comfortable with her way and mine.

That experience reminded me of God's creativity in Genesis. He created the macrocosm (Genesis 1:1-2) and then filled in the details. Homeschooling allows me the freedom to use creative means to do whatever is needed to help my child grow. God's

Spirit, who hovered over the waters, gives us wisdom and discernment. That year I celebrated the creativity and flexibility of homeschooling.

**Digging deeper:** What creative opportunities does homeschooling give you?

# Second-Guessing

"Lord, if it's you," Peter replied, "tell me to come to you on the water." "Come," he said. Then Peter got down out of the boat, walked on the water and came toward Jesus. But when he saw the wind, he was afraid and, beginning to sink, cried out, "Lord, save me!" Immediately Jesus reached out his hand and caught him. "You of little faith," he said, "why did you doubt?" (Matthew 14:28-31)

"Why do you second-guess yourself?" my husband asked as I revisited curricula options. I shrugged and leafed through a curriculum catalog while I stood at our kitchen island. How could I explain the doubts within? Even though, through the seven years of homeschooling, many of them were unfounded, I still second-guessed myself.

It's normal to be concerned about my children's future, but doubts left unchecked can wreak havoc with my mind. Some days, doubts are close companions. My vulnerability depends on many things: tiredness, not-so-good homeschooling days, a scathing remark about homeschoolers, or comparing myself to other homeschooling parents.

I identify too well with Peter, whose heart was gripped with fear when he looked at the storm. At times the swirling winds of doubt overwhelm me, shifting my focus away from the one who said with outstretched arms, "Come, walk this homeschooling path."

Jesus' immediate response in this passage comforts me. His words, "Take courage! It is I. Don't be afraid" (Matthew 14:27), calm the raging winds of fear and doubts. When I cry, "Lord, save me!" his hand immediately grasps mine and pulls me out of the waves of worry and doubt that threaten to overwhelm me. Jesus will do the same for you.

**Digging deeper:** What do Jesus' words in Matthew 14:22-36 mean to you as you homeschool?

# Connecting

May your fountain be blessed, and may you rejoice
in the wife of your youth. (Proverbs 5:18)

Jim reached for my hand as we left the restaurant and walked to our car. A few hours together without feeling like I had various roles to fill had refreshed me.

"I enjoyed the evening." I smiled as I sat back in the car seat. "I wish we could have time like that to chat every day."

He glanced at me as he turned the key in the ignition. "We do."

"When?"

"I call you every evening from the bus! I know it's not as you'd like it, but at least it's something."

I looked out the window. Five-thirty in the evening was not the best time to chat as I rushed to get dinner on the table, often with a toddler attached to my leg. Yet, Jim, knowing how much I needed to "connect" with him emotionally, to feel a part of his day, called me every day on his hour-long ride home. My desire for the perfect time and setting had blinded me to the little windows we had.

*Forgive me, Lord.* I placed my hand over Jim's on the steering wheel.

Those daily calls now are the highlight of my evening. By starting dinner preparations earlier, I am free to chat. When he calls, I leave Katy with Lisa. Sometimes I step into the living room to create a special place where I can talk without distractions. In turn, Jim avoids calling at what he knows are stressful times in the evening.

Not every night can be a date night, so making the most of the minutes together is what's important for any couple.

**Digging deeper:** How do you make the most of windows of time with your spouse?

[ Homeschool and You ] **DAY** 89

# Be Still

"Be still, and know that I am God."
(Psalm 46:10)

*Too busy...*

I knelt beside our aquarium. Its water was a murky mess. Bits of brown, red, and orange flecks performed a slow dance on their way to the bottom. Tiny currents of debris were the only indication of the swimming fish.

"Lisa's the culprit," Jim commented from the sofa. "She knocked over half the fish food because she didn't want to touch it with her fingers."

I gave up following the path of an orange fleck as it disappeared into the swarming mess. *The aquarium mirrors my life. I feel like I'm being swallowed up in a giant vortex of commitments.*

"Give it some time." Jim interrupted my thoughts. "It'll settle down."

Later as I watched the neon orange and blue tetras dart around in the clear water, the verse "Be still and know that I am God" settled into my heart. I suddenly *knew* why I felt overwhelmed. Instead of ceasing from my activities and focusing on the one who called me, I was running deeper into the mire of doing too much. The guilt about thinking I wasn't doing enough, and the times I had agreed to something without praying had all added up. I had lost my focus when I stopped being still before God. It's in the stillness that God speaks and sharpens my focus on what he would have me do.

"Thank you, Lord, for a daughter who thinks touching fish food is gross, and for using a murky aquarium to speak to me," I murmured. "Forgive me. Please align what I think I have to do with what you want me to do. Help me be wise about my time, choices, and commitments."

**Digging deeper:** How does being still before God bring clarity to your schedule? Reflect on 1 Kings 19:9-13.

[ Homeschool and You ] **DAY** 90

# It's Worth It

Therefore . . . stand firm. Let nothing move you. Always give yourselves fully to the work of the Lord, because you know that your labor in the Lord is not in vain.
(1 Corinthians 15:58)

"Lord, sometimes I wonder if we're ever going to make it," I whispered as I rocked Katy. Lisa was adjusting to having a sibling after ten years. I was trying to compensate for the time I had lost with her during my high-risk pregnancy. We were taking a while to get used to a new virtual homeschool program. All combined made for some stressful times at home and school. Close to tears, I continued, "Could you please give me a glimmer of hope today, Lord?"

Later that day I picked up Lisa from a writing test. "I got a narrative prompt, Mama." She skipped to the van. "I had to write about a special person in my life and a special memory," she continued as we drove home. "So I wrote about you."

I looked at her in the rearview mirror. "You wrote about *me*?"

"Yes." She bounced up and down in her seat. "Remember that day Daddy watched Katy? You took me to the mall, and we watched a movie. That's what I wrote about. It was fun."

That one phrase "I wrote about you" drowned out the rest of her chatter all the way home.

As we pulled into the driveway, I remembered a Scripture a friend had quoted to me earlier: "Know that your labor in the Lord is not in vain."

"Thank you, Lord, for glimmers of hope even when life may be hard sometimes. Help me give myself fully to what you lead me to do."

**Digging deeper:** How does 1 Corinthians 5:58 strengthen you as you homeschool?

[ Homeschool and You ] **DAY** 91

# Focus

Let us fix our eyes on Jesus, the pioneer and perfecter of faith. (Hebrews 12:2)

"I can't believe it, Mom." Eleven-year-old Lisa tumbled out of the van. "I'm going to see a president!" She skipped down the pathway to the Carter Center.

Former president Jimmy Carter was autographing a new Habitat for Humanity children's book for which he had penned the foreword.

As we waited in line, I spotted a familiar figure passing through security. She strode in my direction and walked right by wihout noticing me.

"Hi, Kristen," I called.

She paused and then stopped to look around.

"Oh, Anita," she grinned. "I'm sorry I didn't see you. I had my eyes on Chuck," and she gestured toward her husband farther up in the line.

We chatted for a while, but every now and then her eyes would rest on her husband. As we drove home, I thought about the way her eyes kept focusing on her husband, and her words, "I had my eyes on Chuck." I was reminded of Hebrews 12:2: "Let us fix our eyes on Jesus, the pioneer and perfecter of faith."

*What would my life, especially my homeschooling journey, look like if I fixed my eyes on Jesus? How would I handle my doubts and my moments of weakness when I compare myself to others? What about the successes and joys?* When I pulled into the garage, I sat still for a minute and prayed. "Lord, fix my eyes on you. You are the constant on my homeschooling path. You are the one who pioneered it; help me remember that you will perfect it as well."

**Digging deeper:** What does it mean to fix your eyes on Jesus?

# The Role of Homeschool Parents—Part 1

Everyone who competes in the games goes into strict training. (1 Corinthians 9:25)

A virtual program in which we participated for a while referred to homeschooling parents as "learning coaches." That phrase's meaning became clearer after I watched eleven-year-old Lisa's basketball coaches in action.

**Coaches know each athlete's potential.** The basketball coaches knew the strengths and weaknesses of each player. They honed the girls' strengths and challenged their weaknesses, working to bring out the best in each player.

Likewise, learning coaches know their students' God-given potential. God fills each one with wisdom, understanding, knowledge, and skills (Exodus 31:3). What are our children's strengths, weaknesses, learning styles, skills, abilities, and gifts?

As learning coaches, we encourage our children to become all God desires them to be.

**Coaches motivate.** My daughter's team was losing 6–18. "You can't stay down; you gotta be strong," the basketball coaches urged Lisa's team at half-time. In the second half, the girls rallied, and won—26–22.

When we know our children's potential, we can encourage them to develop it for God's glory. Motivating and encouraging are different. While motivating depends on outward means to move a person toward a goal, encouraging focuses more on inner strength. The word *encourage* seems to go hand in hand with the word *strengthen* in the Bible. Both convey a sense of giving courage and developing resoluteness. We point our children to the one who empowers us through his Spirit. When our children stumble, we infuse them with courage. We disciple them into men and women firm in their faith, able to stand strong for righteousness.

**Digging deeper:** How does 1 Corinthians 9:24-27 apply to your homeschool?

[ Homeschool Basics ] **DAY** 93

# The Role of Homeschool Parents—Part 2

They do it to get a crown that will not last, but we do it
to get a crown that will last forever. (1 Corinthians 9:25)

As I watched the coaches through the basketball season, I learned more about my role as a "learning coach."

**Coaches teach the rules of the game and ensure that the athletes abide by them.** We teach our children to run the race of life according to God's Word. The Lord declared of Abraham, "I have chosen him, so that he will direct his children and his household after him to keep the way of the LORD by doing what is right and just" (Genesis 18:19)—that's our responsibility too. Though biblical principles may be counterintuitive to those of the world, we reinforce through our lives and words that living by them *is* the better way.

**Coaches keep their eyes on the prize.** "[Let us fix] our eyes on Jesus, the pioneer and perfecter of faith" (Hebrews 12:2). Keeping our eyes on the one who led us to homeschool helps us stay the path. "He who promised is faithful" (Hebrews 10:23)—that helps us get through the difficult seasons of life and school.

We encourage our children to finish the race and keep the faith (2 Timothy 4:7). Our prize is worth far more than anything the world can offer—"a crown that will last forever" and the words of our Lord, "Well done, good and faithful servant."

**Coaches prepare their athletes to face the sporting event alone.** We train our children and disciple their hearts so they can run the race of life. We know who holds our children in his hands. The God who watches over them does not slumber (Psalm 121:3).

**Digging deeper:** How does Hebrews 12:1-2 strengthen you?

# The Role of Homeschool Parents—Part 3

But commission Joshua, and encourage and strengthen him, for he will lead this people across and will cause them to inherit the land that you will see. (Deuteronomy 3:28)

In this verse, God told Moses to "commission Joshua," who would lead the people of Israel into the Promised Land. As parents, our commission is to prepare our children for life—for the unique role and purpose God has for them.

May God enable us to be coaches who:

**Persevere.** Sometimes it seems as though it takes an eternity for our children to "get it"—academically or with character development. But we can "press on toward the goal" (Philippians 3:14). When we persevere through the not-so good times in life and school, it sends a powerful message of endurance to our children.

**Discern.** "The wise in heart are called discerning, and gracious words promote instruction" (Proverbs 16:21). It's important to know when and how to encourage. Sometimes children need to be challenged. At other times, pushing them may create frustration. Words, a hug, a note, and special times together all go a long way in encouraging.

**Celebrate.** Character never occurred overnight, nor was learning achieved in the blink of an eye. Character building, discipling, and instilling in our children instruction for life is a process. So let's rejoice over the character developing in them. Let's encourage and delight in each step toward the ultimate goal of becoming men and women of God. For we know that our labor in the Lord is not in vain (1 Corinthians 15:58).

**Digging deeper:** How do you prepare your children to run the race of life?

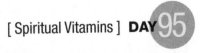

[ Spiritual Vitamins ] **DAY** 95

# Looking Back

See, I am doing a new thing! Now it springs up; do you not perceive it? I am making a way in the wilderness and streams in the wasteland. (Isaiah 43:19)

"Bye, Mama." Nine-year-old Lisa jumped out of the van and hefted her gym bag onto her shoulder. I pressed the button to close the door, smiling as she backed away, waving.

"Watch where you're going," I called. Out of earshot, and before I had time to find a parking space, she walked into the rear of a parked pickup truck. She glanced around to see if anyone was watching. Then she looked at me, and we both burst out laughing.

As I drove away chuckling, it hit me. *Isn't that what I do sometimes?*

I don't always keep pace with the different seasons God has for my life. At times I'm so busy looking back at what has been that I miss what God might have for me. I get so mired in my mistakes, both personal and in our homeschool, that I have a hard time accepting God's promise of a new start. At other times, I'm so focused on the past blessings that I'm loathe to move out of my comfort zone, sometimes even when I sense God's leading. Instead of trust, fear and stubbornness dictate my steps.

Yet God calls us to new life, to new seasons. Though each season may have its challenges, Jesus will not leave us nor forsake us (Deuteronomy 31:6). God will make "a way in the desert" and cause streams to flow in barren land. Jesus is trustworthy.

"Lord, open my eyes to the joys of the new seasons you have for me. Help me trust and follow where you lead."

**Digging deeper:** Into what new seasons might God be leading you? Reflect on Genesis 19:1-29.

[ Homeschool and You ] **DAY** 96

# The Purpose of Homeschooling

Seek first his kingdom and his righteousness, and all these things will be given to you as well. (Matthew 6:33)

What's the purpose of homeschooling? My answers to that question determined our school's direction for a while. As a new homeschooling mom, my Indian background with its strong emphasis on academic excellence directed the purpose of our homeschool—to advance my child academically.

*(handwritten, left margin:)* The real Goal of an education

I believed God had led our family to homeschool, and I had prayed over choices of curricula and activities. But it never occurred to me to pray about what God wanted to accomplish through our homeschool.

These days our school's purpose reflects the God's continuing work in my heart. When I surrendered my will to his, he became the principal of our homeschool.

God's purpose for our homeschool goes far beyond academics. It involves grounding my children in God's Word, nurturing their hearts, and preparing them for life. Homeschooling provides a wealth of opportunities to follow the psalmist's charge, "We will tell the next generation the praiseworthy deeds of the LORD . . . so the next generation [will] know them" (Psalm 78:4,6). While we acknowledge the importance of academics and excellence, our homeschool is now defined by Christ. Our purpose is to encourage our children to draw close to him and to learn how to make him known.

*(handwritten, left margin:)* ✗

I approach school, focusing on "What's God's purpose for our homeschool?" It's that our children "may be encouraged in heart and united in love, so that they may have the full riches of complete understanding, in order that they may know the mystery of God, namely, Christ" (Colossians 2:2).

**Digging deeper:** What's God's purpose for your homeschool? Reflect on Matthew 6:19-34.

# Living Our Dreams ... *(handwritten:)* leading our children to theirs.

Many are the plans in a person's heart, but it is the LORD's purpose that prevails. (Proverbs 19:21)

"Mommy." I looked up from sorting the mail at the kitchen island. Nine-year-old Lisa stood next to me, a drawing pad in her hand. "I want to be a fashion designer."

"You do? What happened to studying medicine?" *I prefer the sound of Dr. Mellott.* As soon as that thought crossed my mind, I traveled back twenty-one years.

My father pulled up at the university's entrance and turned to me.

"Are you sure this is what you want to do?" I nodded and opened the car door.

Before I could step out, he reached for my hand. "Are you doing this for me?" The question hung between us for a few seconds.

He cleared his throat and clarified. "Don't do this exam unless you're sure God's leading you." He was referring to the upcoming entrance test where a few hundred of us would compete for twenty spots in a postgraduate journalism and mass communications program.

"Yes, Daddy."

As I walked toward the room at the end of the dark corridor, I held back my tears. With those words, my father, a well-known figure in communication circles, had released me to soar on the wings of God's purpose for my life.

Now as I glanced at the sketches Lisa thrust into my hands, my cheeks burned. "If that's what God wants you to do, that's fine with me."

"Really, Mommy?" Her grin and sparkling eyes brightened her face.

As I hugged her, I whispered, "Lord, I surrender to you my dreams for my children. May your purpose and plan prevail for their lives."

**Digging deeper:** Whose dreams do your plans for your children reflect? Reflect on Proverbs 16:1-4 and Jeremiah 29:11.

# "Aren't I Too Young to Hear God?"

The LORD came and stood there, calling as at the other times, "Samuel! Samuel!" Then Samuel said, "Speak, for your servant is listening." (1 Samuel 3:10)

"Aren't I too young to ask God what to do with my life?"

I looked down at Lisa's upturned head and serious eyes. So far in her ten years she had wanted to be a doctor, a medical missionary, and a fashion designer. Her question reminded me of Samuel.

Born to Hannah after her many years of infertility, Samuel was a much-prayed-for child. Hannah, overcome with gratitude at God's goodness to her, dedicated her son to the Lord when he was weaned—probably around two or three years old. He ministered in the temple under the supervision of Eli, the head priest.

God called Samuel's name one night and revealed his plans for Eli's irreverent sons.

When Lisa got over her initial shock that Samuel was only twelve years old when he heard God call his name, she thought it was "cool."

God is more than willing to reveal his will for our lives. James encourages us to ask God for wisdom. The Lord "gives generously to all without finding fault" (James 1:5). In Colossians, Paul prays for the believers to grow in the knowledge of God's will (1:9).

Those Scriptures encouraged me and opened the door for my daughter to know that she is never too young to seek God's will or to hear God's voice. All that's needed is an open heart and the willingness to obey.

**Digging deeper:** How do you encourage your children to find God's will for their lives? Reflect on 1 Samuel 1-3.

# It's Okay to Be Different

Do not conform any longer to the pattern of this world, but be transformed by the renewing of your mind. (Romans 12:2)

"Mama." Lisa's brown eyes were solemn. "I'm the only kid in our neighborhood who doesn't go to school." It was something my eight-year-old had become aware of since our relocation to Atlanta.

I drew her into my arms. "You know what? It's okay to be different." And I explained how I had reached that conclusion. . . .

*I'm different.* I noticed it within minutes of entering Frankfurt's airport. Despite my Western clothes, my tan skin and differently accented speech set me apart from the largely Caucasian population. It was a strange feeling after blending in for twenty-five years in India. The feeling intensified when I reached Canada, which was to be home for the next two years while I attended graduate school.

Within months of living in Canada, I learned to embrace my Indian heritage and fit in with North American culture. There was nothing wrong with being different. Sometimes the feeling of being different resurfaces even though I have lived in North America for more than fifteen years.

Human nature is most comfortable fitting in with those around. Yet Paul urges us not to follow the patterns of this world's thinking, but to be transformed by the renewing of our minds. The inner transformation leads to choices, lifestyles, and behavior that differ from those of the world in which we live. When we wear our differences with grace, others see God's light.

Homeschooling parents are all too familiar with the feeling of being different. Our faith-based choices to educate our children run counter to those of mainstream society. As we follow God's unique path for our lives, we're giving our children a wonderful gift: It's okay to live by kingdom principles.

**Digging deeper:** How do you encourage your children to live by a different standard?

# Community

Carry each other's burdens, and in this way you will fulfill the law of Christ. (Galatians 6:2)

"How do you manage everything?" I asked a friend who had stopped by for a few minutes. She balanced, with seeming ease and grace, homeschooling four children, coordinating their various activities, leading our co-op, and being a pastor's wife.

"Oh, Anita." Faint red accentuated her cheeks. "It takes a community to help homeschool."

Her succinct words reminded me how much we need each other.

I can't homeschool in a vacuum, nor can my children live in isolation. Being part of a homeschooling community is vital. The synergy in being with others who share similar journeys and the depth of understanding, compassion, and encouragement they offer is unparalleled.

When I shared with a few homeschooling friends our dilemma about school options for my daughter's upcoming seventh-grade year, they empathized and understood more than my non-homeschooling friends. Their prayer support until my husband and I were in agreement carried me through an uncertain time.

When Lisa had a hard time with some math concepts in sixth grade, several homeschool friends suggested solutions and even offered different curricula for us to try.

During a young mom's battle with cancer, our homeschooling group provided meals, child care, and decorations for her hos-

*I wonder if this could be a substitute for the local church.*

pice room. Moms took turns being with her when her husband was at work.

As a community we carry each other's burdens. By doing so, we're fulfilling the law of Christ—the law of love. "A new command I give you: Love one another. As I have loved you, so you must love one another" (John 13:34). That's what being part of a community is about.

**Digging deeper:** How does being part of a homeschooling community sustain you? Reflect on Acts 2:42-47.

[ Homeschool Basics ] **DAY** 101

# "This Is Impossible!"

His divine power has given us everything
we need for a godly life. (2 Peter 1:3)

"This is impossible, Mom!" I turned to ten-year-old Lisa, who sat staring at her social studies assignment.

"What is it?" Eyes shining with tears, she pushed the book toward me.

"Draw and label a map showing the prairies," I read aloud.

I looked up at her. "It's not that bad. You can . . ." A snapping sound interrupted me. She held up two halves of the pencil she had been gripping under the table. Frustration had gotten the better of her.

We took some time off, during which I researched handling frustration in preteens. I learned that frustration was a common response when something prevented kids from reaching a goal. *Lord, how can I equip her to deal with life's challenges in a godly way?* I wondered, wanting to teach her lessons for life.

Several days later, I read, "His divine power has given us *everything* we need for a godly life" (2 Peter 1:3). As those words sank into my heart, the first step in dealing with Lisa's frustration became clear—to point her to the source of power. God's divine power is mighty. It raised Jesus from the dead (Ephesians 1:19-20) and is available to us to help us live the way God calls us to. Only his power can transform us. Only through his power can we win victory over a challenging situation.

*Lord, thank you that you haven't left me without help as I navigate the ups and downs of homeschool life. Help me teach my children to tap into the power you give us to live godly lives.*

**Digging deeper:** What does being able to tap into God's power mean to you?

# Handling Frustration

Make every effort to add to . . . knowledge, self-control; and to self-control, perseverance; and to perseverance, godliness. (2 Peter 1:5-6)

Jim and I wanted to give Lisa spiritual and practical tools so she could learn how to handle frustration in a godly way.

Second Peter 1:5-6 encouraged us to "make every effort" in dealing with the situation. It also provided the basis for our response by highlighting qualities that were needed in working through frustration.

**Knowledge** or **understanding** helped identify the cause of the frustration—the entire task overwhelmed Lisa. So we broke the assignment into bite-sized pieces and worked step-by-step until the whole map was drawn and labeled.

**Self-control.** Proverbs likens a person without self-control to "a city whose walls are broken through" (Proverbs 25:28). Often I react hastily to Lisa's responses and she to mine, which doesn't help the atmosphere in our school. Self-control had to start with me. When I stepped away from the situation, we were able to be less emotional and gain a better perspective.

Foolish people "give full vent to their rage," but wisdom is shown by keeping oneself under control (Proverbs 29:11). So we discussed appropriate ways for Lisa to express frustration. She could tell me she was frustrated. I encouraged her to take a break to jog or play basketball to channel and expend some of her energy.

**Perseverance** is encouraged through the Bible and is only developed by facing and working through difficulties. At the end of the task, both of us felt better for not giving up.

As we worked through a challenging situation, we were developing self-control, perseverance, and finally, godliness—learning to deal with issues in a manner that honored God.

**Digging deeper:** How can you help your children tap into God's power?

[ Homeschool and You ] **DAY** 103

# "I Don't Need School"

Folly is bound up in the heart of a child, but the rod
of discipline will drive it far away. (Proverbs 22:15)

"Why do I have to do math?" Eight-year-old Evan slammed his palm on the metal desk. His mother, Megan, sighed. *Not again.*

"Can't I only do four problems?"

Megan shook her head, and Evan tossed his pencil down and threw himself against the chair. "I don't need school!"

It wasn't the first time he had complained.

That night his father sat on the side of the bed. "Son," his eyes pinned Evan's. "Your behavior at school is unacceptable. So are your attitudes. We've talked about this before. From tomorrow morning, you'll get up at 6:30, the same time as kids who go to school. I'll leave you some work to finish by breakfast. Let's see how much you like getting up as early as school-going kids."

Evan sighed. "Yes, sir." The punishment that had been talked about was a reality.

Evan gripped his camouflage comforter as they bowed their heads. "God, help my bad attitudes."

The next morning, when Megan came down for breakfast, Evan raced to her. "Mom I did all my reading and math."

She smiled. "See what happens when your attitude's better?"

Over the week, the hand slamming and the complaining eased. By the end of the week, Evan was glad homeschooling meant he didn't have to wake up early each morning. School was smoother, much to Megan's relief.

As parents, our responsibility is to discipline our children even when it's hard. Firm discipline administered in love helps drive foolishness away from our children's hearts.

**Digging deeper:** How do you deal with complaints at school? Reflect on Proverbs 23:13 and Deuteronomy 8:5.

[ Homeschool and You ] **DAY** 104

# Look to the Lord First

God is our refuge and strength, an ever-present help in trouble. (Psalm 46:1)

"I *can't* do this, Mommy." Seven-year-old Lisa's lower lip began to tremble. Her pencil shook and then fell from her hand as she burst into tears.

I drew her into my arms. *Lord, what's going on? She did fine with fractions all year, and now she doesn't know how to add them? Please show me how to help her.*

We set aside math for the day. The next day was no better. At the end of the week, I asked my prayer partner for prayer.

"Anita, have you considered praying with Lisa about math?" Her words pierced my heart. Almost immediately, phrases from my Old Testament readings began to run through my mind. "They inquired of the Lord." "They sought the Lord." I ended my conversation and dropped to my knees. "Lord, forgive me for going to others first rather than to you."

The next day, when Lisa began to shake her head at a math problem, I took her hand in mine. "Let's talk to Jesus about math."

She stared at me and nodded.

After we prayed, not only did she work out the problem, but she finished the whole page without any help from me.

As she waved her paper in front of me, I whispered, "Thank you, Lord, for teaching me to look to you as my strength. Help me come to you first in every situation."

**Digging deeper:** Who do you turn to first when facing times of difficulty? Reflect on Psalms 34 and 46.

[ Homeschool and Family ] **DAY** 105

# The Power of Praise

Encourage one another and build each other up,
just as in fact you are doing. (1 Thessalonians 5:11)

"O holy night . . ." Jim's voice filled the kitchen as I rolled sugar cookie dough at the island. Lisa skipped around, waving cookie cutters, ready for our Christmas tradition.

"I'm Pavarotti!" He bowed with a flourish.

I chuckled. *Right.*

"Oh no, Daddy, you're better than that Pavarotti guy." At my eight-year-old's comment, my cheeks began to burn. I lowered my head and continued rolling the dough, though it was ready to be cut.

*Why can't I be like her? Why does everything have to be perfect to earn praise?*

Later I studied the word "encourage" in 1 Thessalonians 5:11. Its root meaning—"to fortify through providing comfort and reassurance"—seared my heart. I checked the verse in different translations. When I read, "So speak encouraging words to one another. Build up hope" (MSG), I bowed my head. "Lord, help me come alongside my family to build them up and give hope.

When my children need discipline, help me to be gentle and not tear them down."

Opportunities to encourage my family abound—I just need to be intentional about seizing them. It may be complimenting Lisa's effort in school, noticing that she included a child in play group, or praising her for setting the table even though the forks and knives weren't in the right places. Her face lights up and she has a bounce in her step. Thanking my husband for taking the trash out or making a comment about the yard looking good brings a sparkle to his eyes. That's the power of a few simple words of encouragement.

**Digging deeper:** Find a way to encourage your family today. Reflect on Proverbs 12:25.

[ Homeschool and You ] **DAY** 106

# Stress Busters

The human spirit is the lamp of the LORD that sheds light on one's inmost being. (Proverbs 20:27)

A Barna study reported "Compared to the national average, homeschool parents were more likely to say they were 'stressed out' [and] 'too busy.'"* I can relate to being busy—school, co-op, enrichment days, extracurricular activities, and church all add up. I have my share of days when I'm frazzled—whether it's due to school or life. Stress isn't a positive influence on home, school, and me. It steals my peace, leaves me susceptible to health problems, and turns my obedience to God's call into drudgery.

To get a better handle on stress, I decided to figure out its triggers in my life. The answer wasn't easy to come by—it meant being vulnerable before the Lord. When I ask God to search my spirit, my "inmost being" (Proverbs 20:27), he reveals things that rob his joy in my life.

Every few months I spend time prayerfully reflecting on the following questions:

- What causes me the most stress?
- What can I do to change it?
- Where and what can I cut back on or delegate?
- In what areas am I expecting too much of myself or my children?
- When can I take some time away to be refreshed?
- How am I taking care of myself?
- Where can I simplify my life and my homeschool?
- Where is my focus? How can I keep it on Jesus?

*Lord, help me find perfect peace in the midst of all you've called me to do, and to balance with grace the responsibilities with which you've entrusted me.*

**Digging deeper:** Prayerfully reflect on the questions above.

*From www.barna.org/barna-update/article/5-barna-update/57-home-school-families-have-different-backgrounds-than-commonly-assumed.

[ Homeschool and You ] **DAY** 107

# What's Important?

In their hearts humans plan their course, but the
LORD establishes their steps. (Proverbs 16:9)

"Focus on what's important," Jim advised after our second child was born and I felt overwhelmed with our busy schedules. At that point in time, everything seemed important. I read several articles on goal setting and long-term planning but came back to Proverbs 16:9. "Lord," I prayed, "please direct my steps according to what you want me to focus on during this season of my life."

A few days later, I sat down at the kitchen table, divided a sheet of paper into two columns, and labeled them EVERYTHING I DO and EVERYTHING I FEEL GOD IS LEADING ME TO DO. I wrote until I felt my arm would fall off. The items in the second column stood in stark contrast to the first column, which ran onto multiple sheets of paper.

As I reflected on the overflowing column, I began crossing off things that I did out of obligation or guilt. When I reached ten-year-old Lisa's activities, I asked her to choose two. "Sure, Mommy," and she crossed out a few that I didn't even know held no appeal for her.

Finally, I asked Jim to look at my list and highlight what he felt was important to us as a family and for me personally. By the end of the week, my list fit on less than a page.

In the following weeks, I began to reduce activities and finish up commitments in obedience to God's direction. As the weeks lengthened into months, I was less torn and more energetic. Prayerful prioritizing helped gain a heart at peace and gave life to the body (Proverbs 14:30).

**Digging deeper:** How do you prioritize your family's activities and commitments? Reflect on Exodus 18:13-27.

[ Homeschool and You ] **DAY** 108

# Burnout?

Then, because so many people were coming and
going that they did not even have a chance to eat,
he said to them, "Come with me by yourselves
to a quiet place and get some rest." (Mark 6:31)

"I'm so tired when I wake up in the morning, Anita," a homeschooling friend shared over a cup of coffee. "Constantly meeting needs is just getting to me."

I understood all too well. Pregnancy-related health problems a year later were draining me. Some days I was so tired that the tiniest thing sent me into tears. My family skirted around me, which I didn't like.

Both my friend and I were experiencing burnout, which can result from major life changes. Most often, though, it builds up over months of stress, being busy, and not taking care of ourselves.

As I read through Mark, a way to counteract burnout became clear. In chapter 6, Jesus and his disciples were so deluged with people's needs that the disciples didn't even have a chance to eat. Jesus was quick to notice what they needed most—rest (6:32).

So that weekend I rested instead of catching up on housework and errands. We ate peanut butter sandwiches off paper plates, watched movies, and read. My to-do list grew longer that weekend, but I was reenergized.

After enjoying the benefits of rest that weekend, I made it a daily priority. I enforced a "Don't disturb Mom unless it's an emergency" rule and relaxed with a book or music. Once a month I met friends for lunch or coffee. I promised myself not to look at schoolwork after a certain time of the day and asked Jim to hold me accountable. Soon I noticed that where exhaustion depletes, rest rejuvenates and gives a fresh perspective on life.

**Digging deeper:** When was the last time you rested from the busyness in your life? Reflect on Exodus 20:8-11.

[ Homeschool and You ] **DAY**

# Spiritual Refreshing

After leaving them, he went up on
a mountainside to pray. (Mark 6:46)

Imagine slipping away to a quiet spot for some well-deserved rest. You arrive to a waiting crowd. But wait. It's not a welcome party; each one has needs *you* are to meet. That's what happened to Jesus and his disciples when they reached their destination.

When Jesus saw the people, he had compassion on them. I don't know if the disciples stayed while Jesus taught the crowds or not. They came to him later, telling him to dismiss the crowds to get something to eat. That's when Jesus blessed the five loaves and two fish to feed five thousand people and had twelve baskets of food to spare.

After ministering, Jesus went away by himself to pray. As I read this passage, another key to beating exhaustion and stress came to light—taking time to be in God's presence. Sometimes I'm so busy serving through homeschooling that I neglect the one who led me to homeschool.

It's only when I read and meditate on God's Word and take time to sit at Jesus' feet that I am empowered to do all that God leads me to do and my strength is renewed. "Those who hope in the LORD will renew their strength. They will soar on wings like eagles; they will run and not grow weary, they will walk and not be faint" (Isaiah 40:31).

When or how we meet with Jesus doesn't matter. We can have devotions in the afternoon or in the quiet of the night; we can read the Bible or listen to it on CD or an iPod. What matters is taking the time to be with Jesus.

**Digging deeper:** How does being in God's presence refresh and empower you? Reflect on John 15.

[ Spiritual Vitamins ] **DAY** 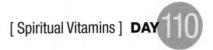110

# Easy Yoke

"Take my yoke upon you. . . . For my yoke is easy
and my burden is light." (Matthew 11:29-30)

I love Matthew 11:28-30. *But how is Jesus' yoke easy and his burden light?* I wondered as images of oxen struggling under the weight of yokes as they plowed the fields in India came to mind. Things became clearer at the gym one day.

As I sweated on the treadmill, my eyes followed a duo entering the gym. The daughter led her mother to the center then climbed onto an elliptical, her gray hair bobbing as she went at a pace I could never hope to achieve.

Her mother shuffled down the aisle and stopped in front of the weight machines. She straightened her bent frame and called one of the trainers.

"Young man, I want to lift some weights." Her trembling finger pointed to a bicep machine.

"Certainly, ma'am." He set the resistance at its lowest.

"Oh, get up. I can do it." Her quavering voice interrupted his demonstration of the machine.

Laughing, he watched her seat herself. Her shaky arms stretched out to grasp the handles. As she lowered them, the trainer moved in behind her and pushed down on the handles so she didn't bear the whole weight herself. A few reps later, she turned around. "Young man, that's too easy. Crank it up!"

Jesus bears the weight of my yoke as he and I walk along the path he's carved out for me. No matter what Jesus calls me to do, he eases its weight. When the going gets tough, Jesus bears the brunt of my sorrows and burdens. He makes the yoke easy and lightens the load.

**Digging deeper:** How does Jesus lighten the weight of your load? Reflect on Isaiah 40:11 and Matthew 11:28-30.

[ Gifts We Give Our Children ] **DAY** 111

# Dependent yet Independent

For you have been my hope, Sovereign LORD,
my confidence since my youth. (Psalm 71:5)

"I'd like to see your math." I wanted to make sure that twelve-year-old Lisa had completed what her tutor had assigned.

"Oh." She stared at me. Her lower lip began to tremble. I was confused. How had I upset her?

"What's the matter?"

"I–It–It's just that I wanted to be independent. I wanted to do math with my tutor."

*How do I hold her accountable without squelching her desire to be independent?* That experience provided the springboard for discussions about independence—something that was becoming important to her.

Independence may be a quality that is applauded in our culture, but for us who follow the Lord, independence is not being apart from God. As homeschoolers, we encourage independence in our children in learning and in preparing for life. But as Lisa is realizing through many discussions, independence is working within boundaries. It is an earned privilege that comes with responsibilities.

Psalm 71 is David's outpouring of dependence on God. A mighty warrior and king, David's strength lay in depending on the Lord. "For you have been my hope, Sovereign LORD, my confidence since my youth" (v. 5). When David wrote this psalm in his old age, he testified that God was his strength throughout his life.

My prayer is that my children, even in their youth, learn that the Lord is the source of their confidence and strength. Independence is not being independent of God; rather, it is relying on him.

**Digging deeper:** What does being independent mean to you? Reflect on Psalm 71.

# Extending Boundaries

The day for building your walls will come, the day
for extending your boundaries. (Micah 7:11)

Different thoughts coursed through my mind at Lisa's comment, "It's just that I wanted to be independent." *How could I honor that desire? Would her schoolwork get done? Isn't it a good thing to develop an independent student? She's responsible with her younger sister; why not give her a chance?*

As I prayed, Micah 7:11 reminded me that the time to extend the boundaries in our homeschool had come. Three principles guided me:

**Define independence.** "What did you mean when you said you wanted to be independent?" I asked Lisa.

"Doing schoolwork alone in my room, Mom."

Jim and I explained that in the Mellott Academy, that was a privilege that went with responsibility and accountability.

**Clear instructions and expectations.** After Lisa's weekly Classical Conversations class, she made a daily schedule, which I reviewed.

- We touched base before and after each subject.
- We created a timed schedule for her to follow.
- She committed to giving me her work for review at the end of each hour and using a timer to keep her on track.
- She was responsible for requesting books from the library for her research papers.

**Rewards and consequences.** When Lisa slipped up on any of the above, she ended up doing school at the kitchen table or going to class with incomplete work.

As we saw Lisa grow in responsibility and accountability, we relaxed some of the rules. For example, she could show me her work after two or three subjects rather than after each subject. And she's developing confidence and character.

Extending the boundaries of our homeschool when the time was right is helping to bring growth and blessings in our home and school.

**Digging deeper:** What do you do to encourage responsibility and independence in your children?

# Letting Go

"I prayed for this child, and the LORD has granted me what
I asked of him. So now I give him to the LORD. For his whole
life he will be given over to the LORD." (1 Samuel 1:27-28)

"Do you have your inhaler?"

Eleven-year-old Lisa nodded as she came downstairs with her
sleeping bag and duffel.

"Let your group leader know if you need anything."

She smiled. "Don't worry, Mom. I'll be fine." We hugged and
waited for friends to pick her up for her first two-day retreat.

I stood in the doorway after they left. *Will it be easier to say good-
bye when she leaves for college?* Somehow I didn't think so. It didn't
matter that she'd been on sleepovers before. I thought of Hannah.
I knew what it meant to pray for years for a child—we'd prayed
for nine years before we had Katy. Did Hannah want to hold on
to Samuel, the child for whom she had pleaded with God year
after year? How did she let him go at such a young age? *Lord,
help me let my children go like Hannah did.*

As I searched 1 Samuel 1 and 2 for Hannah's secret, two truths
emerged:

(1) Hannah's strength lay in the Lord, who had opened her
womb after years of barrenness. "Then Hannah prayed and said:
'. . . in the LORD my horn is lifted high'" (2:1).

(2) She knew to whom she was letting her precious son go.
"He will guard the feet of his faithful servants" (2:9).

As I closed my Bible, a peace filled me. I could let my children
go, knowing God's hands were much bigger than mine.

**Digging deeper:** How does Hannah's example help you in letting
go of your child?

# He'll Catch You

"I will trust and not be afraid." (Isaiah 12:2)

"How do I know you'll catch me?" Seven-year-old Caleb peered down from a tiny ledge five feet off the ground, a deep gorge behind him.

"Look at us," yelled a homeschool co-op buddy. A dozen kids and adults faced each other as their intertwined arms formed a safety net.

Caleb had been the first in line for Trust Fall, a team-building exercise for our co-op kids at camp. Now he took a half step backward, bringing his back up against the solid tree trunk.

"Well, I trust you with my secrets," his voice faltered. "But not to catch me."

"But we're your friends," a chorus of voices replied.

"You can do it, Caleb," the adults encouraged.

He sighed and turned around to face the tree. He closed his eyes, leaned backward, and with clenched fists, dropped off the ledge to our cheers.

Seconds later, a redhead popped up from the carpet of intertwined arms.

"That wasn't too bad." A huge grin spread across his face as he jumped down.

*I'm so much like that*, I thought, as we walked away. I trust God with my deepest longings and struggles. Yet when he leads me to step out, I pull back.

Isaiah 12:2 is a simple but profound reminder that God is trustworthy. The word *trust* implies a place of security. The remainder of the verse gives the reason not to fear: "The LORD, the LORD, is my strength and my song; he has become my salvation." Trusting is a choice to find strength in the Lord. It's faith in action. When God calls, I can leap knowing that "underneath are the everlasting arms" (Deuteronomy 33:27).

**Digging deeper:** Can you leap with abandon into God's arms? Reflect on Psalm 91.

# Dwelling in Safety

In peace I will lie down and sleep, for you alone,
LORD, make me dwell in safety. (Psalm 4:8)

A clap of thunder rattled the house. Lightning illuminated our bedroom through the closed blinds.

"Two seconds," Jim commented, his voice thick with sleep.

Lisa took less than that to burst into our bedroom. She jumped into our bed and pulled the covers over her head as another clap of thunder sounded.

"We need to do something about it," Jim told me the next morning.

"She's only seven."

"I know, but being overtaken by fear isn't good."

That night we read Mark 4:35-40 about Jesus calming the storm. Something flickered in Lisa's eyes when she heard that Jesus slept through the storm until the disciples awoke him.

We prayed and talked about fear, Jesus' power, and his protection.

In the subsequent months, Lisa braved the first few minutes of the thunderstorms alone. Then she ended up in our room with us.

Almost a year later, I came across Psalm 4:8: "In peace I will lie down and sleep, for you alone, LORD, make me dwell in safety."

I showed Lisa the verse during our devotion time. Her face lit up. She took almost half an hour to copy the verse onto a large index card. She took even longer drawing flowers and squiggles around the verse.

I followed her as she ran upstairs. She climbed onto her bed and placed the card on the headboard.

Every night before she went to sleep, she took the card down, read the verse, and prayed. When the first thunderstorm of the season hit, I tiptoed to her room. A flash of lightning illuminated a sleeping figure and the now-faded index card in her hand.

**Digging deeper:** How do you help your children deal with fear? Reflect on Mark 4:35-40.

# Our Father in Heaven

"This, then, is how you should pray:
'Our Father in heaven.'" (Matthew 6:9)

"We're going to learn the Lord's Prayer tonight." Jim sat four-year-old Lisa on his lap. "It's a prayer Jesus taught his disciples. It shows us how to pray."

As we prayed the Lord's Prayer, I found it went beyond guiding my prayer life. It's a treasury of truths that strengthen my faith and help me disciple my children.

With the words, "Our Father in heaven," Jesus offered us an intimate, tender way of approaching God Almighty. The religious leaders of the day considered Jesus sacrilegious and sought to kill him when he referred to God as "his own Father" (John 5:18). Yet we have the privilege of calling God our Father: "The Spirit you received brought about your adoption to sonship. And by him we cry, 'Abba, Father'" (Romans 8:15).

I've often heard that our human parents shape our understanding of our heavenly Parent. But the concept of God as a Father who cares for and loves us transcends what our parents in their humanity could ever offer us.

Crucial to our faith and that of our children's is the understanding and recognition of God as a loving Parent. Only in our faith does the Lord Almighty declare, "I will be a Father to you, and you will be my sons and daughters" (2 Corinthians 6:18). While other faiths view God as a mystical being who needs to be placated, we have a heavenly Father who loves us, welcomes us, and cares so much that he initiated reconciliation.

Our Father God is ready to help us no matter what. He will never let us out of his care.

**Digging deeper:** How does the idea of God as Father affect your relationship with God, with your children, and with your own parents?

# God's Name

"Hallowed be your name." (Matthew 6:9)

With the phrase "Hallowed be your name," Jesus underscores the holiness and reverence associated with the name of God. In Hebrew tradition, names represented the person and had power. Therefore, to call on God's name would be to call on who God is. The Jews held the name of God in such high reverence that they rarely wrote out his whole name or even spoke it.

God inspires awe in those to whom he reveals himself. Afraid, Moses hid his face from God (Exodus 3:5-6). Later, when God delivered the Israelites from the Egyptians and led them through the Red Sea, Moses exclaimed, "Who is like you—majestic in holiness, awesome in glory, working wonders?" (Exodus 15:11). When Isaiah saw God seated on his throne surrounded by the seraphs, he fell face-down and cried, "Woe to me! . . . For my eyes have seen the King, the LORD Almighty" (Isaiah 6:1-5).

The names through which God reveals himself represent different attributes. When I teach my children the names of God, it develops their understanding of God and enables them to call on his power when needed. Some of our favorites are:

*El Roi:* The God who sees me (Genesis 16:13).
*El Shaddai:* God Almighty (Genesis 17:1-2).
*Yahweh\* Yireh:* God will provide (Genesis 22:13-14).
*Yahweh Rophe:* The Lord who heals (Exodus 15:26).
*Yahweh Shalom:* The Lord is peace (Judges 6:24).
*Yahweh Roi:* The Lord is my shepherd (Psalm 23:1).

God is more than enough—call on him. He "is near to all who call on him, to all who call on him in truth" (Psalm 145:18).

**Digging deeper:** Share your favorite name of God with your children. Read *Praying the Names of God* by Ann Spangler.

\*In the past, scholars believed the holy name of God was Jehovah; today they agree *Yahweh* is the best interpretation of YHWH (Exodus 3:13-15).

# God's kingdom

"Your kingdom come." (Matthew 6:10)

"Mom." I glanced at twelve-year-old Lisa as I pulled into our garage. "Umm . . . I have something to tell you."

I parked the van and turned to her. She clenched her hands in her lap. "I've been praying, and I have to tell you this even though it's hard. While you were at the doctor's today, I checked my e-mail even though I hadn't finished school."

I patted her hand. "I'm glad you were honest with me, sweetie."

"Boy, it feels good to tell you." She sighed and slumped in her seat.

That incident reminded me of Jesus' words, "Your kingdom come." Jesus' kingdom is about "righteousness, peace and joy in the Holy Spirit" (Romans 14:17). In his kingdom:

- Faith and surrender are important, not material possessions and wealth (Matthew 19:24).
- Hearts are more important than outward displays of religious practices (Matthew 21:32).
- Entry is through repentance and faith (Mark 1:15).
- Childlike trust is lauded (Mark 10:15) in a kingdom open to all (Luke 4:43).

We have entered this kingdom through believing in Jesus (John 1:12, 3:16). Citizenship in this heavenly kingdom involves living by principles that are not popular in the world in which we live. It involves allowing the King's reign in our lives. As we surrender more to Jesus daily, he becomes preeminent in our lives, transforming us in ways we never would have thought possible.

"You know, Mom," Lisa told me later. "You always tell me not to open the door even a tiny bit to sin, because it may push its way in and fill my heart. But if I let Jesus' light in, it shines brighter and brighter in my heart and pushes out the darkness."

**Digging deeper:** How has God's reign changed your life?

# God's Will

"Your will be done, on earth as it is in heaven."
(Matthew 6:10)

*What does it mean to do God's will on earth as it is in heaven?* I wondered as I studied the Lord's Prayer. Though I found Psalm 103:20, which says the angels do his bidding and "obey his word," my question wasn't fully answered.

Several years later, things became clearer when a homeschooling friend shared with me her family's experience in following God's leading. Megan and her husband, Brad, opened their home to provide a safe place for infants whose families were in crises.

"We're learning that even when you're doing something that God led you to do, it can be hard," Megan said. "It's not easy for our kids sometimes when they have to share me. It's hard to do school some days. And we get so attached to the baby; it's difficult for all of us to give the baby back."

Her words reminded me of Jesus—our perfect example of doing God's will on earth. At Gethsemane, Jesus sweated drops of blood as he wrestled with God's will. Though obedience to the Father's will came at a price—Jesus' life—the results were far-reaching: salvation and peace with God for all who believe in Jesus.

Though God's will is never easy, it can be a place of safety: Daniel was thrown into the lions' den for his faithfulness to God, but God sent an angel to close the lions' mouths (Daniel 6:1-28). As we carry out God's will on earth through homeschooling, we can rest in the assurance that God will keep us until the end.

**Digging deeper:** How can carrying out God's will be a place of rest for you? Reflect on Matthew 7:15-23.

# Our Daily Bread

"Give us today our daily bread." (Matthew 6:11)

*Could this be the Jeff I worked with twelve years ago?* Angie wondered as she noticed his name at the end of an article. Excited to reconnect with a friend and former colleague who was now CEO of a health care company, she called and left a message.

Several days later when he returned her call, they spent more than an hour chatting.

"Angie, do you want a job?"

"But I just told you I homeschool." Her heart began to pound. *Can I go back to the workforce after twelve years? Is this God's provision?* Brian, her husband, had lost his job several months ago.

"We can work that out. We're entering a new market. The position is yours."

"I didn't call to ask for a job." Angie's voice trembled. Though Brian had found another job, it didn't pay as much. The couple had lost a sizable amount of money when the housing market bottomed out. Yet they had felt led to enroll their eldest in a hybrid school without any idea how they would pay for it.

"I *want* you to have this job. You're perfect for it."

Minutes later, tears running down her face, she explained to their three kids what had happened. As they knelt on the kitchen floor, thirteen-year-old Jake reached for his mother's hand. "Mom, you and Dad just finished fasting and praying." Her eyes grew wide.

God had answered their prayers in an unexpected way. He had provided their daily bread and beyond.

**Digging deeper:** Share with your children a time when God supplied your needs.

# Forgiveness

"Forgive us our sins, as we have forgiven those
who sin against us. (Matthew 6:12, NLT)

"I'm looking forward to a quiet evening at home tonight," I commented to a few friends as our toddlers played in the sand at the
park. "It's been almost a week since we were home together."

"Oh, Anita!" a friend exclaimed. "That's *way* too many days
not to be home as a family. I would just tell my kids they couldn't
do so much!"

She probably meant well and only wanted to express concern,
but I felt judged. *How could she say that to me? Doesn't she know how
careful we are with our family time?* I opened my mouth to answer
but decided against it. Jim and I guarded our family time, with
eating supper together every night a high priority. But with basketball makeup games and out-of-town close friends visiting, the
past week had been extra busy.

"Forget it," Jim encouraged me when I shared the incident
with him. "When her kids grow up, she's going to be running
around too."

But her comment stayed with me for a few weeks, even
though I'd heard worse criticisms in the past.

One morning as I read Matthew 6:12, I sighed and said, "Lord,
this is eating away at me. You see my heart, yet you love and forgive me. Help me to forgive too. And please heal the hurt." As I
continued praying that prayer, a slow process began. Rather than
avoiding my friend, I could look her in the eye and smile when
we passed in church. I chatted with her and even looked forward
to getting together. More than that, I didn't feel like there was a
granite wall between God and me.

**Digging deeper:** How does knowing that God forgives you help
you extend that grace to others? Reflect on Matthew 18:22-35.

# It's Hard Not to Do Wrong

"And lead us not into temptation." (Matthew 6:13)

"Mom." I looked up from my book. Eleven-year-old Lisa stood in front of me. "How can I not do the wrong thing? It's so hard sometimes."

I reached for the Bible. "Well, everyone gets tempted." We read James 1:13-14, which clearly shows that when our sinful desires get the better of us, we sin.

"That *doesn't* help, Mom."

"Remember the Lord's Prayer?" She nodded. We recited it together. When we came to "and lead us not into temptation," she stopped.

"See, Lisa? We can ask God to protect us from our evil desires—to help us be aware of evil and resist temptation."

We studied strategies to resist temptation:

**Prayer.** Jesus urged his disciples to "Watch and pray. . . . The spirit is willing, but the flesh is weak" (Matthew 26:41). Prayer invokes God's power and strength in our fight against temptation. We can go to Jesus—he knows and understands our vulnerability and is ready to help. "Because he himself suffered when he was tempted, he is able to help those who are being tempted" (Hebrews 2:18). Even a quick "Help!" suffices.

The **Word of God** is our offensive weapon, as shown when Jesus was tempted after fasting and praying for forty days. For every dart Satan hurled at him, Jesus countered with "It is also written." The Word, God's truth, counters the lies of temptation and strengthens our resistance. So we listed helpful Scriptures for Lisa to memorize.

We discussed **accountability** and let Lisa know she could always call on Jim or me when faced with a difficult situation.

When we ended our study, she smiled. "Mom, of all the verses, 1 Corinthians 10:13 is cool. God won't let me be tempted a bunch. And he'll help me—I just have to ask."

**Digging deeper:** How do you teach your children to resist temptation?

# Deliverance

"...but deliver us from the evil one." (Matthew 6:13)

"Show me your hand," Raj, a university classmate said, grabbing Rohit's hand. "I'll tell you your future."

None of us took Raj seriously with his tall stories. But my initial "Is he for real?" gave way to "I guess he *does* read palms," as Raj told classmate after classmate things about their past that he couldn't have known. Then he predicted their future.

"Anita, come on. See what your future holds," a classmate called.

*There's nothing wrong with seeing what he has to say.* My thoughts pulled me in different directions. *Stay away. It doesn't honor the Lord. What kind of witness will you have?* Then on the other hand, *I want to know if he's right.*

My curiosity won out. As I held out my hand, I whispered, "Sorry, Lord."

Raj peered at my right hand. Then he studied both hands, turning them toward the sunlight.

"What's taking you so long?" one of the girls called.

He dropped my hands, his eyes wide.

"What's wrong, Raj?" I asked.

"What did you do?" his breath came in spurts.

"What are you talking about?"

"Anita, I *can't* see your hand." He began to back away from me. "I–It's like a giant hand has covered yours."

My classmates moved away from me.

Raj stepped up and peered into my eyes. "Did you pray?" As my eyes flickered, he backed away.

I stood alone, relief flooding me. *God had protected me despite my foolishness.*

I had knowingly participated in something that didn't honor God, yet God protected me. How much greater is the Lord's deliverance when we ask for it?

**Digging deeper:** Reflect on a time when God delivered you.

[ Spiritual Vitamins ] **DAY** 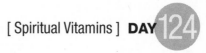124

# God's Kingdom and Power

"... for yours is the kingdom and the power and the glory forever. Amen." (Matthew 6:13, NIV note)

"His kingdom is unstoppable." I read those words under the signature in my friend's e-mail and blinked back tears. *Thank you, Lord, for reminding me that nothing can stand in the way of your kingdom and reign. What an honor to be part of that kingdom!*

I love the ending of the Lord's Prayer, which is a footnote in most Bible versions. Resounding with victory, exultation, and joy, it keeps in the front of my mind some important truths:

- **No matter what comes my way in life or homeschool, I know God is in control.** "The LORD is my light and my salvation—whom shall I fear? The LORD is the stronghold of my life—of whom shall I be afraid?" (Psalm 27:1).
- **I am a victor in the end.** "You, dear children, are from God and have overcome them, because the one who is in you is greater than the one who is in the world" (1 John 4:4).
- **I know who fights for me.** "The battle is the LORD's" (1 Samuel 17:47).

- **I know the outcome.** "In this world you will have trouble. But take heart! I have overcome the world" (John 16:33).

When life sideswipes me, I can stand firm, knowing that my Lord's kingdom *will* come. At the end of my journey through life and homeschool, I can say, "To Jesus be the power, and the glory forever."

**Digging deeper:** How does knowing you're a part of God's unshakable kingdom influence your life and homeschool?

[ Spiritual Vitamins ] **DAY** 125

# Approaching the Throne of Grace

Let us then approach God's throne of grace with confidence, so that we may receive mercy and find grace to help us in our time of need. (Hebrews 4:16)

Eighteen-month-old Katy burst down the hallway. I cautioned, "Don't disturb Nana," and tried to grab her, but she pulled away. She threw open the door to my mother's room and burst in at 6 o'clock in the morning.

"Hi, precious." I heard my mother's voice and a babble of excitement. I peeked in to see Katy enfolded in a hug.

Ever since she could walk, my toddler has raced down the hallway after I get her out of bed. She doesn't knock, nor does she hesitate. She hurtles into the room, knowing my mother's outstretched arms will greet her.

*That's what it means to boldly approach God's throne of grace,* I thought one morning as I watched her. Hebrews 4:16 assures us we can "approach God's throne of grace with confidence." The phrase "with confidence" means boldly, without fear or hesitation. My toddler knew love and outstretched arms awaited her on the other side of the door, and so it is for us in approaching our heavenly Father. His arms are always open. Even when we sin, "we have an advocate with the Father—Jesus Christ, the Righteous One. He is the atoning sacrifice for our sins and not only for ours but also for the sins of the whole world" (1 John 2:1-2). God is always ready to grant grace and mercy in our time of need. Jesus said, "Whoever comes to me I will never drive away" (John 6:37).

**Digging deeper:** How do you approach the throne of grace? Reflect on Hebrews 4:14-16.

[ Homeschool and You ] **DAY** 126

# Wrapped Up

"So now, if the boy is not with us when I go back to your servant my father, and if my father, whose life is closely bound up with the boy's life, sees that the boy isn't there, he will die." (Genesis 44:30-31)

Several homeschooling friends relaxed in my family room as their kids played upstairs.

"I don't know what I'll do when my kids go off to college." A mom glanced upward at the sound of the kids' muffled voices.

"I'm not even thinking of it," said another.

I laughed and pointed to Katy crawling on the carpet. "I have a long time before that happens."

But I encountered it earlier than I thought. About a year later, ten-year-old Lisa attended an all-day, weeklong summer camp. The first few days I'd call her name and then check myself. I felt like part of me was amputated.

As homeschooling parents, our lives are so interwoven with those of our children that it's sometimes hard to separate the two. Jacob knew the feeling. After he lost Joseph, Benjamin became his life.

I drew some comfort from Genesis 44:30-31. *It's okay to feel that way about my kids*, I reasoned. *After all, someone in the Bible did*. But the more I reflected on the verse, a question blazed in my heart: *What would my life be like if it was as wrapped up in Jesus as it is in my kids?* The thought set my cheeks on fire, and I dropped to my knees. "Lord, consume me with your holy passion so my life is completely immersed in you."

**Digging deeper:** What is your life consumed with or wrapped up in? Reflect on Colossians 3:3.

[ Homeschool and Family ] **DAY** 127

# Priorities

The LORD God said, "It is not good for the man to be alone. I will make a helper suitable for him." (Genesis 2:18)

"When do I get some of your time?" Jim asked me.

*How funny.* My initial thought changed as I glanced up from cutting vegetables. He stood next to the island, his shoulders drooping.

"You seem to have time for everything, except me."

I mentally went through my list of responsibilities: home, school, caring for my mother, co-op. . . . My heart plunged when I realized he was right. *But he's an adult. He doesn't need me as much*, I tried to rationalize.

"I know you have a lot on your plate. . . ." His voice trailed off.

Hands trembling, I put the knife down and walked to the sink. As water poured over my hands, I confessed, *I've allowed other responsibilities to cloud my priorities. Lord, please make me be a helper suitable for him.*

I grabbed a kitchen towel and turned to him. "Sorry."

He put his hands on my shoulders. "It's okay."

Since then, we are more intentional about making time for each other. These days, after the kids go to bed, we chat for a while before relaxing in front of the TV or picking up a book, and date night is a priority every week.

Some homeschooling friends shared the following suggestions for spouses:

- Go for a walk together.
- Practice "couch time," where you and your spouse spend fifteen minutes together daily, uninterrupted by kids even though they may be in the same room. It shows children the importance of husband-wife relational time.
- Go out for ice cream or coffee as a family but let the kids sit at a separate table.

The key is to be intentional about prioritizing time for each other.

**Digging deeper:** Reflect on Genesis 2:18-24.

[ Homeschool and You ] **DAY** 128

# Why Aren't They Homeschooling?

Do nothing out of selfish ambition or vain conceit. Rather, in humility value others above yourselves. (Philippians 2:3)

"Hi, Anita. We're looking at school options for our kids, and homeschooling is one. I have so many questions. I'd love your help." My fingers danced over the keyboard as I responded to my cousin's e-mail. That was the beginning of our correspondence about the pros and cons and logistics of homeschooling overseas.

A few months later, my pulse quickened as I read, "After a lot of prayer, we've decided on a private school. It was a hard decision. Thanks for helping so much." *Why aren't they homeschooling?* I wondered. *It would have been perfect for them as trained teachers and missionaries overseas.* Thoughts came and went as I sat in front of the computer trying to process her e-mail. Unable to make my leaden fingers do more than hover over the keyboard, I left to finish some chores.

Over the next few days, I struggled with my response. I wasn't sure how to keep my feelings from coming through. *Why is this so difficult? I wondered. It's their decision. Am I such a die-hard home-schooler?*

I reached for my Bible and turned to Philippians. "Do nothing out of selfish ambition or vain conceit. Rather, in humility value others above yourselves." I traced the words as tears pricked my eyes. I set my Bible aside and dropped to my knees. "Lord, I am so sorry. I thought I was helping, but pride sneaked in. You lead us all in different paths. Help me respect their decision and show them honor. Give me a humble heart as I serve you through homeschooling."

**Digging deeper:** How do you keep from pride in homeschooling creeping in? Reflect on 1 Peter 5:5-6 and Proverbs 22:4.

# Role Model

Have mercy on me, O God, according to your
unfailing love; according to your great compassion
blot out my transgressions. (Psalm 51:1)

"Mama, when I grow up I want to be just like you." Seven-year-old Lisa skipped around our family room dragging me along.

I tried to smile at her, silently praying, *Lord. I'm unworthy of her comment. You know the ugliness inside and how far I fall short of your ways every day. Help me to be a good role model to my children.*

Later I studied the influence of mothers in the Bible, hoping to learn from them. My inadequacies only increased.

How could I match the faith of Jochebed, Moses' mother, who cast her three-month-old adrift in a basket in the Nile? Or of Hannah, who gave her son to the Lord's service at such a young age?

I wanted to emulate Lois and Eunice, who passed their faith down to Timothy and raised him in the knowledge of the Scriptures (2 Timothy 1:5). I desired to submit to God's will, as Mary the mother of Jesus did when she said, "May it be to me as you have said" (Luke 1:38).

Finally, I ended up on my knees and began to pray through Psalm 51. I paused at verse 3. "Lord, 'I *know* my transgressions, and my sin is always before me.' How can I ever hope to live up to her trust in me?"

*On your knees at the foot of the cross,* came the answer, breathing hope into my heart.

"Help me, Lord, always to see my need for you and to point my children to the cross," has been my prayer since then.

**Digging deeper:** What does the cross mean to you as you disciple your children?

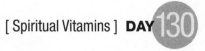

[ Spiritual Vitamins ] **DAY** 130

# Love's Covering

Love covers over a multitude of sins. (1 Peter 4:8)

I ran my fingers over the crisp pages of my Mother's Day gift—a new Bible to replace my tattered twenty-year-old one. *I'm going to take better care of this Bible,* I determined. *Maybe it'll last longer than the other one.*

A few weeks later, I placed it on my nightstand after my devotions. As I stood up, my hand brushed against a glass of water. I watched in horror as the pages turned into a soggy mess. I grabbed a towel from the bathroom, wrapped the dripping Bible in it, and ran downstairs.

*You're so careless. You've ruined a new Bible. So much for it lasting a long time.* My thoughts accused me as I opened the door to the sunroom. I lay the Bible on a wicker chair and dragged it to the spot that got the most sun.

Throughout the day I checked on my Bible, my heart sinking every time I saw its drooping, wet pages.

That night I stood in the sunroom looking at the warped water-wrinkled pages of my Bible. *Go buy a new Bible. This one's no good. It's a reminder of your carelessness.* Perfectionism battled with relief that my Bible was still usable. *It's fine. It's not that damaged. I can still use it.*

I picked it up and turned it over, feeling the bumpiness of the pages. *Child, I love you just the way you are,* a whisper floated into my heart.

Over the years, I've come to treasure that Bible. It has become a cherished reminder that God's love covers the multitude of my imperfections.

**Digging deeper:** What does God's perfect love mean to you? Reflect on Psalm 136.

[ Homeschool Foundations ] **DAY** 131

# Homeschool Lessons from Jesus

To this you were called, because Christ suffered for you, leaving you an example, that you should follow in his steps. (1 Peter 2:21)

First Peter 2:21 lays down a daunting challenge—to follow in Jesus' footsteps. It forms the foundation of Charles Sheldon's book *In His Steps*, in which a pastor dares his congregation to live by the question, "What would Jesus do?" That question has lingered in my mind ever since I read the book as a teenager.

The Gospels reveal some vital principles from Jesus' life on earth that can be applied to homeschooling. We'll look at a few in this and the following entries.

Jesus knew his purpose. From the early age of twelve when he questioned Mary and Joseph, "Didn't you know I had to be in my Father's house?" (Luke 2:49), right through his last days on earth, Jesus knew his work was to do the will of his Father (John 4:34, 6:38). It helped him stay the path, even through the darkest valley. In Gethsemane, as he faced the raw agony of his impending death, he cried, "My Father, if it is possible, may this cup be taken from me. Yet not as I will, but as you will" (Matthew 26:39). Jesus bore the weight of the sins of the world, faithful to the end to his Father's will.

On the not-so-easy homeschooling days, we can stand firm because the one who called us is faithful. The knowledge that God has led us to nurture the hearts of our children focuses us and keeps us resolute. Through the storms, we can say our hearts are steadfast because God promises to restore us and make us strong, firm, and steadfast (1 Peter 5:10).

**Digging deeper:** Read *In His Steps* by Charles Sheldon.

[ Homeschool Foundations ] **DAY** 132

# Depending on the Father
## Homeschool Lessons from Jesus

"The Father is greater than I." (John 14:28)

While Jesus walked this earth, his commitment to his relationship with his Father in heaven offers some important truths for home-schooling parents.

Jesus declared, "I and the Father are one" (John 10:30). Why then did he seek to keep in close communion with his Father? Because throughout his ministry on earth, Jesus reiterated that "the Son can do nothing by himself" (John 5:19). Jesus spoke and did only what his Father taught (John 8:28).

If the Son of God looked to his Father so much, how much more I need to do so each homeschool day. Only by depending on Jesus can I accomplish all that he leads me to do. Only by remaining in him can we have any impact (John 15:5).

Jesus' closeness with the Father not only kept him fixed on his purpose on earth, but it also helped him live a life in balance. He knew all about being busy. Despite the grueling demands on him, he spent time alone with his Father (Matthew 14:13, Mark 1:35, Luke 4:42). Jesus knew that his relationship with the Father was integral to his ministry, and he took the time to nurture it.

The key to homeschooling well is depending on the Lord completely. Vital to our ability to do his will through homeschooling our children is taking time for prayer, worship, and the study of God's Word. By seeking "first his kingdom and his righteousness" (Matthew 6:33), we keep our focus on him and what is important.

**Digging deeper:** What do you do to nurture your relationship with the Lord? Reflect on John 14.

[ Homeschool Foundations ] **DAY** 133

# Serving:
## Homeschool Lessons from Jesus

"I have set you an example that you should do as I have done for you." (John 13:15)

Jesus' earthly life reveals some important insights in the area of serving that we can apply to homeschooling.

Jesus lived a life of service. He met needs regardless of whether he was recognized or thanked. Whether it was healing, teaching, or raising someone from the dead, he poured himself out for others. For "the Son of Man did not come to be served, but to serve, and to give his life as a ransom for many" (Matthew 20:28). Jesus fulfilled his ultimate act of service on the cross. Today he serves as our High Priest, advocating on our behalf (Hebrews 2:17).

Jesus said, "Whoever serves me must follow me" (John 12:26). We serve him through homeschooling, as we give of ourselves to our families, to others in the homeschool community, and to the larger community in which we live.

Jesus' service meant taking time for people. Wherever he went, crowds followed him—some curious, others skeptical, and some faithful followers. A touch here, a word of hope there, or a look of love, Jesus never seemed rushed. Some days Jesus ministered through the night, yet he always had time for people.

This challenges me. I can get so caught up in my schedules and the work I'm called to do that I sometimes miss opportunities to be there for my children and to reach out to others. I may miss an opportunity for a hug, a word of encouragement, or playtime with my children. Or I may miss ministering to others with an e-mail, a phone call, a meal, or a note to say "I'm thinking of you." To serve is to be Jesus' hands and feet.

**Digging deeper:** How does your homeschool reflect the Master's example of serving? Reflect on John 13:1-17.

[ Homeschool Foundations ] **DAY** 134

# Unconditional Love
## Homeschool Lessons from Jesus

"For God so loved the world that he gave his one and only Son, that whoever believes in him shall not perish but have eternal life." (John 3:16)

Jesus' life of love offers valuable lessons that we can apply to our homeschool.

Just as Jesus is God's gift of love, our gift of love to our children is homeschooling.

God took the first step by giving us Jesus—even when we were still lost in sin (Romans 5:8). When we were most unlovable, love sent him to the cross. His love makes us what we are today and covers our sins. It's something worth remembering when offenses and hurt feelings over correcting our children spill over from school into home and vice versa, souring the sweetness of relationships. That's when we can take the first step toward forgiveness and to bring peace and unity in our school and home.

That's the kind of love our children need from us. No matter what they've done, whether they've worked as they should or not, we are to love them, accept them, and hold them close to our heart. Sometimes we may inadvertently communicate that love is dependent on their performance. But Christ's love for us is unconditional. "Dear friends, let us love one another, for love comes from God. Everyone who loves has been born of God and knows God" (1 John 4:7). Love is a better way.

**Digging deeper:** How is love displayed in your homeschool? Reflect on 1 John 4:7-21.

# Obedience:
## Homeschool Lessons from Jesus

"I have come down from heaven not to do my will but to do the will of him who sent me." (John 6:38)

As I followed Jesus' life in the Gospels, it became clear that his purpose was to obey the Father. No matter what came his way on that path—criticism, not being accepted by the community—he still obeyed the Father. That encourages me daily as I homeschool.

Jesus' obedience cost. He lived his life on earth in the shadow of the cross. Though Jesus knew the end would be brutal, he followed through with his Father's will. "Being found in appearance as a man, he humbled himself and became obedient to death—even death on a cross! Therefore God exalted him to the highest place and gave him the name that is above every name" (Philippians 2:8-9).

Homeschooling costs in some way or another—a career, an extra income, a dream put on hold, the approval of a loved one, or the discomfort of being considered strange. But nothing can compare to the rewards of obeying God's leading. The joy of seeing our children growing into men and women who love Jesus and stand up for righteousness, and of having the satisfaction of knowing we consistently obeyed our Lord, is incomparable. "We fix our eyes not on what is seen, but on what is unseen, since what is seen is temporary, but what is unseen is eternal" (2 Corinthians 4:18-19).

**Digging deeper:** How has your obedience to homeschool been worth it so far for your family? Reflect on Psalm 103.

[ Gifts We Give Our Children ] **DAY** 136

# The Power of Jesus' Name

Some trust in chariots and some in horses, but we trust in the name of the LORD our God. (Psalm 20:7)

Four-year-old Lisa burst into our bedroom. She scrambled onto the bed and buried her head in my chest.

"I–I'm sc–sc–scared." I held her close until her sobs subsided.

"Did you have a bad dream?"

I felt her nod. My arms tightened around her.

After snuggling for a while, she pulled away.

"You can sleep here tonight, or we can pray and you can go back to your room."

Thoughtful brown eyes peered through wet eyelashes. "I'll pray and go to my bed."

"Are you sure?"

Her black-brown curls bobbed at her nod.

After our prayer, still holding her hand, I knelt down and looked her in the eye. "Jesus' name has power. Whenever you're afraid, you can call on his name. Do you understand?" Another nod.

We walked across the living room and down the hallway to her room. I kissed her and drew the blanket over her. Leaving her bedroom door slightly ajar, I lingered in the hallway and then settled into the sofa in the living room.

Sniffles and soft sobs roused me. I tiptoed to her room.

Ready to push the door open, Lisa's voice stopped me. "J–J–Jesus, Mommy said you can h–h–help me." A few hiccups. Silence. "In the name of Jesus," her voice rose to a crescendo, "bad dreams go away!"

Later that night when I checked on her, she was sound asleep.

**Digging deeper:** When did calling on the name of Jesus help you? Take some time to share that with your children today. Reflect on Psalm 20.

[ Homeschool and Family ] **DAY** 137

# Prayer in Spiritual Warfare

Finally, be strong in the Lord and in his mighty power.
Put on the full armor of God so that you can take your
stand against the devil's schemes. (Ephesians 6:10-11)

"I need to battle for my kids," a homeschooling friend told me in the course of conversation one day. At the time, I didn't pay much attention to her reference to spiritual warfare. *After all,* I reasoned, *I pray for my children daily.*

Almost a year later when our family began to navigate the tricky waters of adolescence, God engraved the truth of her statement on my heart.

God searches for intercessors to "stand . . . in the gap" (Ezekiel 22:30). As parents, interceding for our children is our responsibility. We intercede for them to grow into mature men and women of God, and to protect our family from the attacks of the enemy.

Spiritual warfare is a reality (Ephesians 6). So Paul urges us to "be alert and always keep on praying" (v. 18). Alertness is imperative in battle since we don't know when or how the enemy will strike. Prayer helps guard against the wiles of the enemy and puts a hedge of protection around us and our children.

How can we *always* keep on praying?

Be open to the Holy Spirit's prompting as God brings people or situations to mind for prayer. Obey the prompting to pray whether it makes sense or not. We don't need to know the details of the situation. Simple prayers of a few words can suffice. What is important is to pray. Use verses to help anchor faith in your heart. Scripture can bring peace, comfort, and assurance.

**Digging deeper:** How do you intercede for your family and friends? Reflect on 1 Thessalonians 5:17.

[ Spiritual Vitamins ] **DAY** 138

# The Power of Prayer

Devote yourselves to prayer, being watchful and thankful. (Colossians 4:2)

As I wrestle in prayer for my children that they "may stand firm in all the will of God, mature and fully assured" (Colossians 4:12), sometimes I'm at a loss to articulate my heart to God. In those moments, I'm assured that "the Spirit helps us in our weakness. We do not know what we ought to pray for, but the Spirit himself intercedes for us through wordless groans. And he who searches our hearts knows the mind of the Spirit, because the Spirit intercedes . . . in accordance with the will of God" (Romans 8:25-27).

When the answers to my prayers are long in coming, or when they come in ways I don't want or expect, I get battle-weary. That's when I experience the blessings of being part of a community of believers.

Praying with others brings:

**Comfort.** We comfort others with the reassurance we received from God during our troubles (2 Corinthians 1:3-4). There's comfort in knowing someone has my back.

**Strength.** Friends may not have all the details of the issues, yet they stand strong on my behalf. Their faith infuses me with strength. Two are better than one, Scripture tells us, because if one of us falls down, a friend will help us up (Ecclesiastes 4:9-10).

**The power of Christ's presence in our midst.** "I tell you that if two of you on earth agree about anything they ask for, it will be done for them by my Father in heaven. For where two or three gather in my name, there am I with them" (Matthew 18:19-20).

**Digging deeper:** Reflect on the verses above and a time when you experienced the blessings of others praying for you.

[ Homeschool Foundations ] **DAY** 139

# On the Same Page

"Do all that you have in mind," his armor-bearer said.
"Go ahead; I am with you heart and soul." (1 Samuel 14:7)

"I want to homeschool, but my husband isn't keen on it. I feel so torn," a friend shared with me. I knew exactly how she felt. I had waited for more than a year before Jim decided that homeschooling was right for our family. Agreement between spouses about homeschooling is one of the cornerstones for successful homeschooling.

"So what should I do?" she asked.

I shared my experience with her and promised to pray for her family.

**Pray for discernment and guidance.** "I am your servant; give me discernment" (Psalm 119:125). Ask God to help you discern his leading for your family. "Teach me to do your will . . . ; may your good Spirit lead me on level ground" (Psalm 143:10). Ask God to lead both you and your spouse in his paths. He doesn't usually speak to one and not the other.

**Trust and don't depend on your own understanding** (Proverbs 3:5). It's tempting to take things into our own hands by trying to convince our spouse or by continually bringing up the issue. God doesn't need our help. He is more than able to bring about what he desires.

**Wait on the Lord and put aside anxiety.** "Be still before the LORD and wait patiently for him" (Psalm 37:7). His timing is perfect.

A year and a half later, my friend called me. "Anita, you can stop praying now. We're going to homeschool in the fall!" I smiled. God *does* "make everything beautiful in its time" (Ecclesiastes 3:11).

**Digging deeper:** Reflect on a time when you waited for God's timing. What were the results?

[ Gifts We Give Our Children ]  **DAY** 140

# The Blessing of Openness

I urge, then, first of all, that petitions, prayers, intercession and thanksgiving be made for all people. (1 Timothy 2:1)

"Please pray for me to be a good leader at work," Jim shared as we sat around the family room one Sunday evening.

Eight-year-old Lisa looked up from her doll.

"You need prayer, Daddy?"

At his nod, she turned to me. "You too, Mommy?"

"Of course I do, sweetie."

"Does that mean you have problems?"

Jim moved closer and put his arm around her. "All of us have problems. That's why we pray. We need Jesus' help."

"We can help each other by praying," I added.

She bent her head and began twisting her doll's hair. "Please pray that I won't be afraid tonight," she whispered.

Jim and I glanced at each other over her head.

Since our relocation to Atlanta, she had nightmares. Though we had talked to her about moving, prayed about it, and decorated her room to replicate the one she had left, she ended up in our room almost every night. Still she refused to talk about what was bothering her.

Jim and I decided to share a prayer request every week, hoping it would help Lisa see our need for Jesus. We regrouped at the end of each week to discuss how God had helped us. Several weeks later, Jim shared that he was better able to prioritize and focus on his staff's needs. Lisa smiled. "I can sleep better now."

First Timothy 2:1 encourages us to pray for others, and James 5:16 encourages us to be open so we can support each other in prayer. Those times of sharing and prayer are strengthening our family and our faith.

**Digging deeper:** Reflect on James 5:16. How does sharing with and praying for each other encourage your family?

# Who Am I?

Since, then, you have been raised with Christ,
set your hearts on things above, where Christ is
seated at the right hand of God. (Colossians 3:1)

"Homeschooling's not working," Jim informed me one evening.

My heart began to pound. "What do you mean?"

"Whenever you and Lisa argue at school, it stresses you out."

I looked away. The last few months had been hard as our pre-teen, Lisa, began to assert herself and her independence.

"You should consider putting her in school in the fall."

"Because of *one* bad year?"

"I'm worried about you." He reached for my hand. "She'll be fine at school."

We agreed to pray for guidance—Jim about continuing to homeschool, and me for openness to other school options. Despite our commitment to pray, Jim's words bothered me.

In the following weeks, I struggled with anger, hurt, feelings of failure, and betrayal that Jim would consider putting Lisa in school. *What about us homeschooling through high school? He's right—homeschooling isn't helping my relationship with Lisa. Lord, I want your will—what is it?*

Several weeks later, I still couldn't shake the pain at his words. *Lord, why do I hurt so much?*

I pulled out my Bible after a sleepless night. My eyes blurred when I read, "Set your heart on things above, where Christ is seated at the right hand of God." What had begun as an act of obedience to the Lord—homeschooling—had developed into more than that. Homeschooling defined me.

"Forgive me, Lord," I prayed as I knelt next to the bed. "Please set my heart on you and the things of your kingdom. Be my security and confidence."

**Digging deeper:** What defines you? Reflect on Matthew 6:19-24.

# It's Not Working

Even there your hand will guide me, your right
hand will hold me fast. (Psalm 139:10)

*"I'm worried about the stress you're under. Homeschooling's not work-*
*ing. Lisa needs a mom more than a teacher."* Jim's words echoed in
my mind.

With the beginnings of adolescence, Lisa and I clashed at
school and home. In addition, role reversal with an aging mother
in our home was changing our family dynamic. Jim was concerned about my emotional stress. His solution was to send Lisa
to school. I wasn't there yet.

*Failure. You're abandoning her when she needs you most. You couldn't*
*make it to the end.* My thoughts mocked me. "Lord," I whispered in
the dark, "should we stop homeschooling?"

My pulse still racing, I opened my Bible to Psalm 139. Its familiar words both became my prayer and pierced my heart, bringing
revelation. "You have searched me, LORD, and you know me"
(v. 1). *Lord, you know my fears of letting go.*

"You are familiar with all my ways. . . . You hem me in behind
and before, you lay your hand upon me" (vv. 3,5). *I can't hide from*
*you, Lord. Lead me in your ways.*

By the time I reached verse 12, my heart's erratic rhythm had
settled. "The darkness will not be dark to you; the night will
shine like the day, for darkness is as light to you." In my darkness, God's light would illuminate the path we were to take.
Jesus loved Lisa even more than we did. Whatever the path, we
could trust that the Shepherd knew the way.

"Thank you Lord, that you know the way. Even though it may
not be the way I'd like to take, I trust you."

**Digging deeper:** Reflect on Psalm 139.

# Because You Say So

He said to Simon, "Put out into deep water, and let down
the nets for a catch." Simon answered, "Master, we've
worked hard all night and haven't caught anything. But
because you say so, I will let down the nets." (Luke 5:4-5)

"Anita, I'm okay with continuing homeschooling." Jim's eyes
searched mine. "I think you're taking on a lot, but I'll support
you in this decision."

I sagged into the sofa, relieved.

After months of prayer and discussion, we had reached a decision about Lisa's upcoming seventh-grade year. But worry soon
got the upper hand. *What if Jim was right about taking on too much?*
*What if I couldn't balance home and school well?* Over the last few
months, I had felt torn between everyone's needs and what I
could give. The challenges of our past school year concerned me.
I had no guarantee that the new one would be better.

As I read Luke one morning, Simon's response when Jesus
told him to cast his fishing nets in again captivated me. "Master,
we've worked hard all night and haven't caught anything. But
because you say so, I will let down the nets." The phrase "But
because you say so" wrapped itself around my heart. *Did Simon*
*want to cast his nets again after a hard night's work? Did it make sense?*
*Yet he obeyed.*

I bowed my head. "Lord, I don't feel like I have much to show
for the past school year. My net is empty." I hesitated. "But
because you say so, I'll cast it in another year."

Following God's leading isn't always easy, but my obedience
mattered despite whether what he told me to do made sense or
not. Jesus would take care of the rest.

**Digging deeper:** What does the phrase "because you say so"
mean to you? Reflect on Luke 5:1-11.

# When You Obey

He and all his companions were astonished
at the catch of fish they had taken. (Luke 5:9)

"Lord, you know I felt like my net was empty last year, but I'm thankful for a new homeschool year. I commit it and us into your hands. Thanks for being with us." I prayed as Lisa came downstairs with her backpack, ready for her first day of seventh grade with Classical Conversations.

Eighteen weeks later, her words tumbled out. "Is this really the last day of my first semester, Mom? I *love* CC!"

I reflected on her comment throughout the day. We've had our difficult moments during school, but working within her learning style has renewed her love for learning. Each day is peppered with snippets of her newly discovered knowledge.

After returning from her first day of class, she threw up her hands. "I can't believe they expect *me* to break down a whole week of schoolwork!" By the middle of the semester, she commented, "I can't believe how easy it is to make a schedule, Mom." She's showing diligence as she tackles Latin for the first time and learns to map the countries and capitals of the world from memory. Working with a tutor is developing more confidence in her for math and sparking an interest in the subject.

Above all, as she reads apologetics books and memorizes catechism, her questions about faith are shifting from, "How do I know what I believe is true?" to "How can I *not* believe that?" Laughter rings out during school rather than arguments. Our mother-daughter relationship is being strengthened through the beginnings of adolescence.

I blinked back tears and whispered, "Lord, sometimes it's hard to follow your leading, but I'm amazed and humbled at how full our net is. Thank you."

**Digging deeper:** How has God surprised you when you obey his leading?

# Childlike Trust

"Do not let your hearts be troubled. You believe
in God; believe also in me." (John 14:1)

"Anita?" My best friend's voice sounded hollow and tinny over
the phone at 10:30 p.m.

"Yes." I felt my heart pounding as fear about the time of the
call from India gripped me. "What happened?"

"Your Dad died a little while ago." Hearing those words, at the
age of thirty-three, my life changed forever.

The next few days blurred as the news sank in and we got
visas processed. Ten days later we were en route to India, but by
then I had missed my father's funeral.

I watched two-year-old Lisa as she sat on Jim's lap on the
plane, playing with a toy the flight attendant had given her. Later
she stood wide-eyed as I showed her the Alps through the nurs-
ery window at Zurich's airport. When we reached India, she
smiled at family and friends, some unfamiliar to her yet dear to
me. She gasped at the beggars and the cows on the streets. *Her little world's been turned upside down, yet she's unafraid. It's because she
trusts us,* I thought. As that truth sank in, a verse settled in my
heart, "Do not let your hearts be troubled. You believe in God;
believe also in me" (John 14:1).

"Lord," I prayed as I hesitated on the threshold of my parents'
home, "my heart is distressed." I felt Jim's hand on my back—
gentle, yet urging me to enter. "Help me trust you like a little
child." I stepped into the living room, and my eyes fell on my
father's chair. I swallowed a lump in my throat. "Jesus, I'm so
glad you are with me."

**Digging deeper:** What does it mean to trust God like a child?
Reflect on Psalm 56:3-4,10-11 and Isaiah 12:2.

# Relationships

"'Love the Lord your God with all your heart and with all
your soul and with all your mind.' . . . 'Love your neighbor
as yourself.'" (Matthew 22:37-39)

"Lord, this passage reinforces that you're all about relationships."
A tear slid onto my Bible. "I didn't know the preteen years could
be so tough."

The beginnings of adolescence brought a subtle shift in my
relationship with Lisa. I found it harder to choose my battles
wisely as peer opinions and asserting herself were increasing in
importance for her.

Rather than helping, homeschooling complicated our relationship. The times we argued over school issues overshadowed the
good times. "Please show me how to build a better relationship
with her, Lord." My tears fell freely.

*Child, are you loving her as yourself?* The whisper in my heart
jolted me. As I reread Matthew 22:39, the answer was clear: I
needed to show Lisa that I loved her for herself—not for who I
wanted her to become.

Over the following months, I didn't confront Lisa unless she
committed a deliberate act of disobedience. I looked for ways to
connect with her even if it involved things that didn't interest me,
like discussing fashion trends or the subtleties of various shades
of nail polish.

Over a year later, I pulled into the church parking lot.

"Aren't you coming in, Mom?"

"Yes, but you go on in. I know you like your independence."

"It's silly for us to go in separately."

When I hung back a bit, she matched her pace to mine. "Mom,
I *want* to walk with you."

We entered church together. As I watched her run upstairs to
her Bible study, my heart overflowed. "Lord, thank you that you

are a God of relationships. Through love, you reconcile us to you and to each other."

**Digging deeper:** How do you focus on relationships with your children, especially during difficult times?

# Time

And this is love: that we walk in obedience to his commands. As you have heard from the beginning, his command is that you walk in love. (2 John 1:6)

Eighteen-month-old Katy ran to me as I entered the family room. LEGO blocks from the tower she and my mother had built scattered all over the carpet. She pulled me toward the staircase and sat on the bottom step. Then she patted the place beside her and handed me a Pooh Bear book.

*She wants me to spend time with her.* I was amazed. I had only been a few feet away at the kitchen table working on grammar with Lisa for half an hour.

Sometimes people ask me, "Why do you want to spend one-on-one time with your kids when you're with them all day?" My answer: Because quality time in the midst of quantity of time makes a real difference. One-on-one time with my children spells love.

Since I'm with my kids almost all day, it's challenging to make daily time with each of them a priority. Some days I'm successful; others I'm not. But when I "walk in love," carving out time for my children becomes a priority.

So when Lisa plops on the sofa next to me after I've put Katy down for a nap, love causes me to put aside my desire to relax and I focus on my preteen. When I've risen early for some alone time and Katy decides she's ready for her day, love calls me to snuggle on the sofa as she has her milk.

Walking in love sometimes calls for sacrifices. Jesus, who personified love in its truest form, helps me put aside my agenda to be a channel of his love to my family.

**Digging deeper:** How is true love shown in your homeschool and family life? Reflect on Ephesians 5:1-2.

[ Homeschool and Family ] **DAY** 148

# Intentional Communication

And now these three remain: faith, hope and love.
But the greatest of these is love. (1 Corinthians 13:13)

The aroma of freshly baked muffins filled the kitchen. I smiled as I put them on a plate for breakfast. I enjoy baking. It's one of the ways I show my family love.

"Um, Anita." Jim entered the kitchen as I carried the muffins to the table. "I . . . I'm not sure how to say this." He ran a hand through his hair and blurted, "You know what? I really don't like banana muffins."

"What?" I almost dropped the plate. "But I've been baking them for eight years!"

Often, people communicate love in the way they would like to be shown it, but that doesn't always mean it's the way the other person would like to receive love. Finding meaningful ways to communicate love and respect daily to each other goes a long way in strengthening a marriage.

Through our sixteen years of marriage, Jim has learned that bringing me a morning cup of coffee or helping me clean the house communicates more to me than a bouquet of flowers or an "I love you" card. He knows that giving me time to browse in a bookstore or treating me to a latté means more to me than a shopping spree. I know that sending him off with his friends for a movie or football game without putting a guilt trip on him about time away from family is like treating him to a steak dinner. A compliment about the yard and help in keeping the house clutter-free speaks volumes to him. And I've discovered since then that Jim prefers banana-nut bread instead of muffins!

**Digging deeper:** Read the book *The Five Love Languages* by Dr. Gary Chapman.

[ Homeschool and Family ] **DAY** 149

# No Regrets

Be very careful, then, how you live—not as unwise but as wise, making the most of every opportunity. (Ephesians 5:15-16)

The tears I had been holding back gave way to a smile as my friend's beaming face filled the TV screen. My dread at attending her wake dissipated with each photo of the slideshow.

I remembered my last visit. She lay on a hospital bed. Her two elementary-aged boys' drawings decorated the bedroom walls.

"I won't see them graduate or marry, but I want them to remember me." Her bony hands clutched the book in which she was writing a letter to each of them for every year until they turned eighteen.

Now the slideshow and scrapbooks chronicling her years with her family eased the pain of that visit. They evoked memories of the full-of-life kind of person she was, who loved nothing more than enjoying her family and friends.

As I hugged her husband, I realized she had lived her short years on earth to the fullest. And that reinforced my desire to treasure each moment I had. Ephesians 5:15-16 reminds me to be "very careful" how I live.

Our lives have a certain measure. I want to seize every opportunity to delight in my kids and enjoy each stage. No moment can be recaptured, but the memories linger.

Sometimes academics, schedules, or getting things done hold me captive. I miss out on moments in life that can become sweet memories—like Katy's delight in bathing the house in light when she discovered she could reach the switches or even Lisa's discovery of yet *another* way to do her hair.

I want to live in the joy of each moment, even if it is ordinary.

**Digging deeper:** How do you make the most of every moment?

[ Homeschool and You ] **DAY** 150

# The faithfulness of God

He who began a good work in you will carry it on to completion until the day of Christ Jesus. (Philippians 1:6)

I slumped in my seat at church, hoping I could keep my eyes open through the service. The nights of interrupted sleep with an ill baby and the challenges of the last few weeks had caught up with me. What was it about decimals and fractions that made Lisa stare at me as if I were speaking a foreign language? Why were chores so hard to remember when she didn't have to be reminded about a friend's visit? Why was it that when I had a break-through in one area of my life, another issue popped up? *Will we ever get it, Lord?*

I sat up straight as the morning speaker, Dr. John Haggai, founder of Haggai Institute for Advanced Leadership Training, said, "Don't let the enormity of the task smother you." *That's just what I needed to hear, Lord. Thank you.*

Homeschooling and parenting can be daunting responsibilities. When I look at myself and my frailties, when I see the gap between my longing to be conformed into God's image and where I am, dejection can engulf me.

Yet, as always, Scripture is my comfort. Philippians 1:6 offers hope. It's a promise that the Lord *will be* faithful to complete the work he's started in my life. Jesus doesn't grow weary of my many issues and struggles. Whenever I stumble and fall, he's quick to reach out, pull me up, and walk beside me, his hand in mine. As I lean on him, Jesus will empower me to extend that same grace to my children.

**Digging deeper:** What reassurance do 2 Corinthians 12:9 and Isaiah 40:29 offer you in homeschooling and parenting?

[ And a Child Will Lead Them ] **DAY** 151

# Safe Families

"The King will reply, 'Truly I tell you, whatever you did for one of the least of these brothers and sisters of mine, you did for me.'" (Matthew 25:40)

Megan saw the hope and longing in her husband, Brad's, eyes as they watched a documentary about adoption during their church's missions week.

The minute the lights came on, six-year-old Erin and eight-year-old Evan grabbed Megan's hands and squealed. "Mommy, can we get one?" Before she could answer, their attention turned to a second video about the Safe Families for Children ministry. As Megan watched stories of families who provided a safe place for infants and children whose families were in crises, various thoughts went though her mind. *Was this why we haven't been able to have other children? Would this ease the ache of wanting another child? God has blessed us. We can take care of another child.* She felt a tug toward the ministry that provided a safe haven for children during family crises.

"Let's pray about it," she answered her kids.

After a few weeks of prayer, this homeschooling family began the process to become a safe family for infants from birth through six months.

Seven months later, Megan picked up an infant whose mother needed some time to get a job and a decent place to live.

Over the next six months, they cared for four infants.

"Both our kids are all over the babies," Megan commented. "They help as much as they can. It's been good for our family. My kids now know that serving others goes beyond taking a few cans of food to church. If it wasn't for our own kids, we may not be doing this today."

**Digging deeper:** What might God be leading your family to do? Reflect on Matthew 25:31-41.

[ Gifts We Give Our Children ] **DAY** 152

# A Safe Harbor

Sons are a heritage from the LORD, children
a reward from him. (Psalm 127:3-5)

Lights dimmed for a video about families in our church who had opened their hearts and homes to orphans.

The camera zoomed in on two teenagers. As their story unfolded, I blinked back tears and glanced at ten-year-old Lisa. Her eyes were cast down.

Taken from an abusive situation, the sisters went from foster home to foster home until they ended up in the care of a family at our church who adopted them. Until then they had never known what it was like to feel safe and be loved.

On our way home, Lisa interrupted our conversation. "Are there really families like the one the girls grew up in?"

Jim looked in the rearview mirror. "Yes."

The rest of the ride home was devoid of her usual chatter as she sat staring out the window.

Through the day, the sisters' story lingered in my mind.

Psalm 127:3 speaks of children as a blessing from the Lord. God has entrusted them to us to be cherished and raised in his knowledge and reverence. As parents we give children the gift of a safe family—a secure place where love is present and where they can be themselves—a place where open communication and strong family ties are encouraged. Families are to be harbors of safety for our children. We are to raise our children in love, not embitter them (Colossians 3:21).

May our children always know what it is to grow up in a family where they are cherished and nurtured.

**Digging deeper:** In what ways do you communicate love and acceptance to your children? Reflect on Psalm 127.

[ Homeschool and You ] **DAY** 153

# A Labor of Love

Do everything in love. (1 Corinthians 16:14)

"Every day is a labor of love filled with prayer." My friend Anne looked at me over her cup of coffee. Tears shimmered in her eyes as she described the joys and challenges of homeschooling a special needs child.

"You and I don't think of all the thought processes that go into something as simple as writing the letter *L.* I have to teach her how to hold a pencil, demonstrate what the lines look like, and hold her hand as we write the letter."

Anne drew a deep breath. "The next day, we start all over because she's forgotten. It's challenging to find new ways to go over the same thing with her. By the end of the day, I'm emotionally and physically spent.

"A special needs child changes the family dynamic. We need support, especially my other kids as siblings of a special needs child. They think she's the favorite because of all the attention. So we deal with that as well."

Anne grew animated. "I'd love for someone to offer to watch the kids, but sometimes people shy away because we have a special needs child. Often all we get is pity. But there's no time for self-pity." She sat straighter in the chair, and her eyes began to sparkle. "We didn't know she would have Down syndrome. My husband said we were blessed to have someone so special in our family."

As I watched Anne drive away, I whispered, "Lord, forgive me for being so caught up in my own homeschooling world. Show me how I can help other homeschooling families."

**Digging deeper:** How does being a part of a community of homeschoolers encourage you to reach out to other families? Reflect on Philippians 2:4.

[ And a Child Will Lead Them ] **DAY** 154

# Giving from the Heart

If your gift is . . . giving, then give generously. (Romans 12:6-8)

"Mama, I want to help Miss Lilly."

I smiled and patted seven-year-old Lisa's head.

Miss Lilly, an eighty-year-old widow in our church, had been the victim of identity theft by her son. With her bank account wiped out and credit cards maxed, she couldn't pay her bills, let alone the debt that he had run up.

"I want to give her my money," Lisa persisted.

"How much, sweetie?"

"*My* money, Mama." Her voice rose. "My five dollars." I dropped the duster. *That's all she has.* She had been saving to buy an outfit for her American Girl doll.

I knelt and looked into her eyes. "Are you sure?"

She nodded.

The next day, she handed an envelope to Miss Lilly, who gasped as the five-dollar bill fell onto her lap. She stared at it and picked it up with trembling fingers. She turned to my daughter. "Is this yours?"

"It's yours now." She pressed herself against me.

"I can't take this," Miss Lilly's voice quavered.

"But I want you to have it."

Miss Lilly drew her into a bear hug. "I'm going to frame this," she declared, her eyes wet with tears. "It's too precious to use."

As we left the low-income apartment complex, my daughter skipped to the van.

"Sweetie, was that hard to do?"

She paused, head tilted. "When I gave it to her, it was. But then I was happy."

The word *generous* means to give sincerely, from the heart. I had been blessed to see such generosity in action.

**Digging deeper:** Reflect on Mark 12:41-48.

[ Gifts We Give Our Children ] **DAY** 155

# Our Worth

This is love: not that we loved God, but that he loved us and sent his Son as an atoning sacrifice for our sins. (1 John 4:10)

"Mom, I don't think she likes me." Eleven-year-old Lisa's eyes followed me as I washed vegetables. "Every time I get online and IM her, she gets offline."

I put the cutting board on the counter and turned to her. "Are you sure?"

She nodded, her brown eyes serious. "Even when she sees me she's not very friendly."

I walked over to her and put my arm around her. "I'm sorry, sweetie. I know it hurts. It's a hard lesson . . . but not everyone you meet is going to like you."

She looked down.

"Daddy and I love you, and there's someone who loves you always, even more than you can imagine. You're so precious that Jesus died for you so you could live."

Human nature craves acceptance. When we perceive the opposite taking place, it gnaws at us despite the friends we already have. For tweens and teens, peer acceptance grows in importance.

Sometimes it's hard for our kids to comprehend the depth of God's love and acceptance, and that his love can be a place of rest. The tangibility of God's Word is a powerful balm of truth. We wrote down a few verses to help her:

- She is God's child (John 1:12; Galatians 3:26).
- She is part of a chosen people (1 Peter 2:9).
- The Lord is her constant (Deuteronomy 31:6).
- God's love for her is everlasting (Jeremiah 31:3).
- God has engraved her on the palms of his hands (Isaiah 49:16).
- God will never forget her (Isaiah 49:15).

**Digging deeper:** Affirm your love for your children. Share the verses above with your children.

[ Homeschool and You ]  **DAY** 156

# It's Not about Me

If anyone serves, they should do so with the strength God provides, so that in all things God may be praised through Jesus Christ. To him be the glory and the power for ever and ever. Amen. (1 Peter 4:11)

My voice faltered as I read 1 Peter 4:11 before school. I fixed my eyes on the pages as my mind flashed back to several weeks earlier.

My heart pounded as my seven-year-old opened her Iowa Test booklet. Our prayer time hadn't calmed my racing pulse at her first standardized test.

Things didn't get easier. I cringed when her pencil hovered over the little circles. When she gazed out the window, I bit my tongue to keep from nagging about a timed test. Whenever I read a question and her eyes glazed over, my heart sank.

Through the weeks that followed that stressful day, I wondered why I had been so uptight. Now my answer stared me in the face: homeschooling wasn't about me—it was about serving the Lord and Lisa to his glory. But I had wanted to be validated as a teacher by her performance.

"Mama?" My daughter snapped me back to reality. "What's wrong?"

Eyes still cast down, I shook my head.

"Mama, you look ill."

I reached up to touch my cheeks, sure that they were red.

"Remember when you took your test a few weeks ago?" I held her gaze. "I'm sorry I was so tense. I know it bothered you. I was more concerned about the results than making you feel comfortable. Will you forgive me?" She nodded.

Before we started school, I whispered, "Lord, empty me of my desires for validation and approval so that you alone are glorified."

**Digging deeper:** How do you react when your children are taking tests? Reflect on 1 Peter 4:7-11.

[ Homeschool and You ] **DAY** 157

# Casting an Image

"You did not desert them, even when they cast for themselves an image of a calf and said, 'This is your god, who brought you up out of Egypt.'" (Nehemiah 9:18)

My heart beat faster as I skimmed Lisa's Iowa Test scores.

"Yes!" I squealed and ran into the house, waving the paper over my head. After homeschooling for two years, she had taken a standardized test.

I reveled in the results all summer and couldn't wait for our new school year to begin.

After the first few weeks of school, something gnawed at the back of my mind. *Lisa's working hard, and we enjoy school, so what's wrong?* Yet I couldn't shake the feeling that something wasn't right.

I prayed through the next few days, asking God to show me what was weighing me down.

Several weeks later, I took an afternoon to polish our brass Indian artifacts. I smiled when a vase's dullness gave way to a bright sheen. As I ran my fingers across the shiny surface, a verse came to mind. "They cast for themselves an image of a calf and said, 'This is your god, who brought you up out of Egypt.'" My heart began to pound, and the blood rushed to my face.

My delight in Lisa's results had grown into an image that I had cast for myself—success for which I thought I was responsible. My heart had grown proud, and I had forgotten the Lord (Deuteronomy 8:13-14).

I blinked back my tears as I whispered, "Lord, forgive my pride. Help me boast in you and you alone" (Psalm 44:8).

**Digging deeper:** How can you guard from pride creeping into your homeschooling? Reflect on Deuteronomy 8:10-18.

[ Homeschool and You ] **DAY** 158

# The Voices

Therefore, there is now no condemnation for those who are in Christ Jesus. (Romans 8:1)

*You don't do enough with your kids. You should look better for your husband. You should volunteer more.*

The voices in my head accuse and condemn. Their whispers crescendo and gnaw away at the abundant life Jesus promised. Insecurities, inadequacies, and comparisons set them off. Their root lies in my vulnerability to guilt.

Jesus came to loosen my shackles of guilt and condemnation—to set me free to "run in the path of [his] commands" (Psalm 119:32). I take tiny steps toward that daily as I:

**Weigh the whispers against the truth of God's Word.** "For the word of the LORD is right and true" (Psalm 33:4). If the whispers don't align with Scripture, they are from the enemy. When I brandish the sword of the Spirit, the Word of God, his truth silences the accuser of the soul.

**Accept forgiveness.** God promises, "If we confess our sins, he is faithful and just and will forgive us our sins and purify us from all unrighteousness" (1 John 1:9). I need to accept and live in his forgiveness. Sometimes I write what's weighing me down. As I shred it into minuscule pieces, a weight lifts off my shoulders.

**Live like it.** Truth is stronger than feelings. I have to believe I'm forgiven before I feel like it. I pray, "Guide me in your truth and teach me, for you are God my Savior, and my hope is in you all day long" (Psalm 25:5).

"It is for freedom that Christ has set us free. Stand firm, then, and do not let yourselves be burdened again by a yoke of slavery" (Galatians 5:1).

**Digging deeper:** What reassurance do the verses in Colossians 1:21-23 offer you?

[ Spiritual Vitamins ] **DAY** 159

# God's Voice

My sheep listen to my voice; I know them,
and they follow me. (John 10:27)

"Here she is." My OB/GYN held up our second daughter. Then within minutes, nurses whisked her off to the NICU.

"Fluid in her lungs," they told me. "We'll bring her to you in a little while."

Several hours later, I awoke from my anesthesia-induced sleep to see my husband cradling our baby. He came over and placed her in my arms.

"Oh, how cute she is!" I exclaimed, holding her.

At the sound of my voice, the little bundle in my arms squirmed. Her head moved in the direction of my voice.

At my "Hi, baby, it's good to see you at last," her eyes fluttered open, and she gazed at me. Then with a sigh, she closed her eyes and snuggled into my chest. My heart melted when I realized she had recognized my voice.

Jesus said, "My sheep listen to my voice and follow me." But before we can obey him, we need to be able to hear what he has to say. How can we recognize the gentle voice of our Savior in the clamor of the voices vying for our attention in the world?

"Remain in me, as I also remain in you," declares Jesus (John 15:4). We abide in him by immersing ourselves in his Word, seeking him, and losing ourselves in worship. The better we know Jesus, the easier it becomes to recognize his voice. Though other voices may get our attention because we're conditioned to respond to our name, we are to "run away . . . because [we] do not recognize a stranger's voice" (John 10:5).

*Lord, give me ears to hear you calling my name.*

**Digging deeper:** Reflect on John 10:1-18.

[ Homeschool and You ] **DAY** 160

# Homeschool and Work?

She considers a field and buys it; out of her
earnings she plants a vineyard. . . . She makes
linen garments and sells them, and supplies the
merchants with sashes. (Proverbs 31:16,24)

"You homeschool and *work*?" I nodded and smiled at the homeschool mom I had just met. She pursed her lips and turned away.

*Am I less of a homeschool mom because I work? Would it matter if she knew I worked part-time and from home?* I wondered on my drive home after the meeting. *Am I short-changing my kids? Should I stop doing what I enjoy—writing?*

When I got home, I turned to Proverbs 31:10-28 hoping that familiar passage about a "wife of noble character" could shed some light on my struggle.

I was surprised at what I learned:

**She was an enterprising woman.** Not only did she run her home and care for her family, but she was a businesswoman who earned money. Relief seeped in—I wasn't doing anything wrong by working.

**Her husband had confidence in her** (v. 11) **and praised her** (v. 28). He supported her, and apparently they were in agreement about her various roles.

Verse 16 brought things into perspective: "She considers a [new] field before she buys or accepts it [expanding prudently and not courting neglect of her present duties by assuming other duties]" (AMP). She was prudent, carefully considering her time and commitments before taking on new duties. She didn't neglect her family in the midst of all she did.

As I closed my Bible, I prayed: "Lord, help me always to seek and stay within your will for my life. Please keep my priorities right so that I don't work to the neglect of my family." That prayer still brings freedom and peace.

**Digging deeper:** Reflect on Proverbs 31:10-28.

[ Gifts We Give Our Children ] **DAY** 161

# Success?

Yet when I surveyed all that my hands had done and what I had toiled to achieve, everything was meaningless, a chasing after the wind; nothing was gained under the sun. (Ecclesiastes 2:11)

Eight-year-old Lisa gasped at the carved teakwood front door of my friend's new house in India. Our awe grew at the marble pillars, murals on the walls commissioned by famous artists, and ornate furnishings.

"They must be very rich, Mommy," Lisa blurted after their chauffeur saw us to my parents' condo. "I wonder how it would be to live like that." She closed her eyes.

"Is that what life's about, sweetie?" She frowned at my question.

That led to discussions about success as we visited friends ranging from the wealthy to the missionary who fed homeless street kids and had suffered for the name of Jesus.

Kingdom principles aren't easy to teach to our children in the face of different societal values. But true success isn't merely about riches, fame, and influence. Jesus declared, "Truly I tell you, it is hard for someone who is rich to enter the kingdom of heaven" (Matthew 19:23). Ecclesiastes 2:11 indicates the emptiness of the trappings of success. The preceding verse says, "I denied myself nothing my eyes desired; I refused my heart no pleasure" (Ecclesiastes 2:10)—yet the biblical author found everything meaningless. Meaning comes from knowing Jesus and setting our hearts to follow him (2 Chronicles 26:5; Psalm 1:1,3; Matthew 6:33). Obedience to God is linked to success—the Israelites were commanded to obey God's commands and decrees that it might "go well" with them and their children (Deuteronomy 4:40, 6:3,18).

Jesus said that if we love him, we will keep his commands (John 14:23). That's "success" enough.

**Digging deeper:** What concept of success do you teach your children? Reflect on Ecclesiastes 2.

# True Success

Observe what the LORD your God requires: Walk in
obedience to him, and keep his decrees and commands,
his laws and regulations . . . so that you may prosper
in all you do and wherever you go. (1 Kings 2:3)

"I don't understand, Mama. Why would my Grandpa not want
such a huge house?" Lisa turned to me in the cab as I showed her
the sprawling bungalow in which I had grown up in India.

"You know what? I didn't understand either when I was
eighteen. I missed the chauffeur-driven cars and the maids. I was
mad at Grandpa for a long time." Using my father's life as an
example, we focused on what true success meant to those who
follow Jesus.

**Seeking God's will is paramount.** "Grandpa loved his job in
advertising and didn't want to leave it. But as he prayed, he realized God wanted him in ministry (Psalm 37:4). When Grandpa
obeyed, those years were the most fulfilling years of his life."

**There's nothing wrong with material success.** It's our attitudes that matter. "At one point in time, Grandpa said that success blinded him to his need for God (Deuteronomy 32:15). So, he
decided to use what God had blessed him with to help others."

**Success can't always be counted in terms of lifestyle bless-
ings.** "When Grandpa left advertising, he didn't earn as much,
but he found joy in obeying Jesus. Now, eight years after he died,
you still hear people talk about how God used him to touch their
lives."

True success is doing God's will—though we may not understand it and it doesn't make sense. It had taken over twenty years
and my father's life and death to show that to me.

**Digging deeper:** What does success mean to you?

# Homeschool Success

Keep this Book of the Law always on your lips;
meditate on it day and night, so that you may be
careful to do everything written in it. Then you will
be prosperous and successful. (Joshua 1:8)

Relief flooded me at the end of our first year of middle school. We had finished our curriculum, and Lisa's standardized scores were good. Later in the summer, however, I began to wonder, *What does homeschooling success look like?*

As I prayed and studied success, two things became clear: (1) Success has everything to do with God's hand on our lives (Genesis 39:2, 2 Chronicles 26:5). And (2) Success goes far beyond accomplishments and material blessings. It's about having Jesus at the core of our being, walking in his ways, with God's Word as our compass (Joshua 1:8).

With that in mind, success in our homeschool now means:

- We take time to build relationships with God and each other.
- Our children are taking steps toward making godly, wise choices and standing up for righteousness.
- Our family is a safe place for our children, where we affirm them and work through problems in a healthy way.
- We focus on discipling our children's hearts.
- Our children feel they can come to us with any question or problem.
- Our children are moving toward becoming independent learners.
- Our children are pursuing wisdom and can apply knowledge.

**Digging deeper:** What does homeschool success look like to you? Reflect on Psalm 1.

# Doors Homeschooling Opens

Pray for us, too, that God may open a door
for our message, so that we may proclaim
the mystery of Christ. (Colossians 4:3)

"Is your daughter here to see the doctor?" A voice drifted across
the waiting room. "Um, no ma'am." I glanced up and turned my
attention back to our math work sheets.

"Then why isn't she in school?"

"I homeschool." I braced for the onslaught.

"Oh, how wonderful!"

I immediately warmed to the elderly lady in the ophthalmolo-
gist's office.

The questions about homeschooling kept coming, but I didn't
mind. Soon others joined in the discussion.

When the nurse called her name, Mrs. Stroman gave me her
phone number. "Please come see me, dear."

We did a few weeks later. Widowed for more than twenty
years, without children, and legally blind, she spent her days in a
nursing home. Her laughter filled the room as my seven-year-old
entertained her with *Curious George* and *Amelia Bedelia* stories. We
traveled back to the early 1900s as Mrs. Stroman recounted stories of her childhood in Boston. In the months that followed, we
visited her almost every week. Those afternoons became our
highlight. Several years later, when we broke the news of our
relocation to Atlanta, tears trickled down her weathered cheeks.

Through the years, homeschooling has offered opportunities
I never could have imagined. Curious employees at a standardized test venue, customers in grocery stores, passengers on
transatlantic flights, people at parties, all without exception
ask, "Why do you homeschool?" Without fail, our faith-based

answer leads to more questions, usually about faith. Home-schooling has opened doors of opportunity to share the hope only Jesus can bring.

**Digging deeper:** How has homeschooling helped you reach out to others?

# Blessings

The blessing of the LORD brings wealth,
without painful toil for it. (Proverbs 10:22)

"I think you should put Katy in day care a couple of times a week," my friend commented as she looked at me over her menu. "That way you can have some time for yourself."

I couldn't hold back my grin. "I'm a homeschooling mom, remember? My kids are around 24/7, and I love it!"

"But isn't it a sacrifice?"

When I left the restaurant, her question was still ringing in my ears. Then images of our homeschooling years flashed through my mind: Lisa sitting on my lap as we sounded out her first let-ters. The grin that lit up her face as she read, "The cat sat on the mat," her little index finger pressed on mine as we followed the words. Her furrowed brow as she held up tiny fingers while try-ing to figure out an addition problem. Our exhilaration when we jumped up and down, cheering at the end of each school year. Her delight when she took breaks in her school day to play with her little sister. Katy finding *A* among the alphabet magnets on the fridge and calling for Lisa the minute she woke up.

Yes, homeschooling costs—I hadn't been able to pursue a full-time career, and some days there were other things I'd like to do with my time. But the joy of being home with my girls and being a part of each stage of their lives was a blessing that far outweighed the temporal benefits. I had neither sorrow nor regret over our homeschooling decision.

**Digging deeper:** Reflect on some of your special homeschooling moments and 2 Corinthians 4:18.

# Decisions

I will instruct you and teach you in the way you should go;
I will counsel you with my loving eye on you. (Psalm 32:8)

*What should we do about our next school year?* Jesus indicates the wisdom of exploring and considering options before making a decision: "Suppose one of you wants to build a tower. Won't you first sit down and estimate the cost to see if you have enough money to complete it?" (Luke 14:28). That advice is the basis of our decision-making process.

**Evaluate.** By the end of our first semester, Jim and I begin praying about our next school year. By the middle of the second semester, we evaluate our current school year and explore various options. When Lisa entered middle school, in addition to reviewing curricula, we attended open houses for science homeschool classes, and hybrid school options so we could make informed decisions. Lisa's feedback is important as she grows older.

**Consider your family's needs.** Katy's birth changed the way we did school. I couldn't give Lisa all my time and attention. We worked around Katy. The amount of time available for extracurricular activities changed as well.

**Make decisions that are best for your family.** Each homeschool is unique with choices depending on God's leading. In seventh grade, Lisa began Classical Conversations. We stopped attending a homeschool co-op and cut down on her extracurricular activities to focus on a rigorous curriculum.

Conscious that our information is nothing without God's wisdom, we lay our options at Jesus' feet and "be still before the LORD and wait patiently for him" (Psalm 37:7). Some years our decisions have been easy to make. Other years it has taken longer than I'd like, with much time spent on our knees.

One thing is sure—as today's verse promises—God *will* show us the way no matter how long it takes before peace comes about a certain direction.

**Digging deeper:** What reassurance do James 1:5-7 and Isaiah 30:21 offer for your homeschooling decisions?

[ Homeschool Foundations ]  **DAY** 167

# The Spiritual Side of Decision-Making

Trust in the LORD with all your heart and lean not on
your own understanding; in all your ways submit to him,
and he will make your paths straight. (Proverbs 3:5-6)

All my year-end evaluations, information gathering, and lists of the pros and cons of various options fall flat in the absence of seeking God's wisdom and guidance. No matter how overwhelmed I may be with homeschooling decisions, the burden always lightens when I'm on my knees.

Over the years, I've learned the following:

**An open mind is essential.** We desire God's will for our homeschool, which requires openness to his leading and not depending on my own wisdom (Proverb 3:5). One year I was certain a particular option would work well for us. But when we explored it more, I walked away disappointed. I need to remember that God's ways and thoughts are not mine. They are much higher and better (see Isaiah 55:8-9).

**Surrender and trust go hand in hand.** Committing my ways to the Lord (Psalm 37:5) means surrendering my plans—what I think is best. It's the key to trusting God with "all my heart." When I abandon my will to his, I'm saying, "Yes, Lord, you know best. Show me and I will follow you."

**Prayer underscores every decision.** Sometimes the answer is quick in coming; other times it takes a while. During the latter times, I have to hang on in faith, knowing that in God's time, he will show us the way. Though I like to make decisions well in advance, I've found over the years that God's timing is best.

**Digging deeper:** How does the knowledge that God knows the answers help guide your homeschooling decisions? Reflect on Psalm 37:3-7.

[ Gifts We Give Our Children ] **DAY** 168

# Praying the Word— Part 1

"... so is my word that goes out from my mouth: It will not return to me empty, but will accomplish what I desire and achieve the purpose for which I sent it." (Isaiah 55:11)

"Anita, ask the Lord to lead you to a verse for each of your children. Pray that for them," advised a pastor when I began to intercede in earnest for my children. "I just pray chunks of Scripture over my kids and grandkids," offered another friend.

Since then, I personalize Scripture to pray over my children.

**Faith.** "Lord, let their faith be personal. Don't let them be carried away by strange teachings. Let them be your people, and please, Lord, be their God" (see Ezekiel 18:20, Hebrews 13:9).

**Future.** "Lord, lead them into your paths for their lives. May they be open to your plans and your will. For you know the plans you have for them, plans to prosper and not harm them, plans to give them hope and a future" (see Jeremiah 29:11).

**Hearts.** "Lord God, let their hearts be tender toward you and your Word. Let them desire the things of your kingdom. Give them a new heart and a new spirit. Put your Spirit in them and move them to follow your decrees and keep your laws" (see Ezekiel 36:25-27).

**Attractions.** "God, don't let them be conformed to the pattern of this world. Transform them by the renewing of their minds" (see Romans 12:2).

**Resisting temptation.** "Let them submit to you, Lord. Help them resist the devil, and cause him to flee from them" (see James 4:7). "Help them to hate what is evil and cling to what is good" (see Romans 12:9).

**Digging deeper:** How does Scripture guide your prayers? Reflect on Psalm 119:9-16.

[ Gifts We Give Our Children ] **DAY** 169

# Praying the Word— Part 2

For the word of God is alive and active. . . . It penetrates even to dividing soul and spirit, joints and marrow; it judges the thoughts and attitudes of the heart. (Hebrews 4:12)

As I heeded my friends' advice, I discovered that praying God's Word over my children strengthens my prayer journey and brings comfort, guidance, and peace. And Scripture covers *every* aspect of their lives:

**Spiritual growth.** "I keep asking that the God of our Lord Jesus Christ, the glorious Father, may give you the Spirit of wisdom and revelation, so that you may know him better. I pray also that the eyes of your heart may be enlightened in order that you may know the hope to which he has called you" (Ephesians 1:17-18).

**Discernment.** "And this is my prayer: that your love may abound more and more in knowledge and depth of insight, so that you may be able to discern what is best and may be pure and blameless for the day of Christ" (Philippians 1:9-11).

As my children grow older, I encourage them to pray Scriptures that will guide them through life:

**Purity.** "Above all else, guard your heart, for everything you do flows from it" (Proverbs 4:23). "Pursue righteousness, godliness, faith, love, endurance and gentleness" (1 Timothy 6:11).

**Choices.** "Blessed is the one who does not walk in step with the wicked or stand in the way that sinners take or sit in the company of mockers, but whose delight is in the law of the LORD, and who meditates on his law day and night" (Psalm 1:1-2).

There's power in praying God's Word.

**Digging deeper:** Read the book *The Power of a Praying Parent* by Stormie Omartian.

[ Gifts We Give Our Children ] **DAY** 170

# Of Greater Worth

"Indeed, the very hairs of your head are all numbered. Don't be afraid; you are worth more than many sparrows." (Luke 12:7)

"Do you like my hair, Mama?"

"Yes." I glanced up from the computer screen as nine-year-old Lisa tossed her head, sending her thick black curls in an arc through the air.

"Oh. I wish I had straight hair and that it was browner."

It wasn't the first time she had brought up the topic.

"Lord, give me wisdom," I prayed as I walked toward her. "Don't you like the way you look?"

She didn't meet my gaze.

"God created you." I put my hands on her shoulders. "God doesn't make mistakes." A tiny tear glinted on her eyelash. "Every hair on your head is numbered."

Her eyes grew wide. "It is?"

I opened the Bible to Luke and read, "Are not five sparrows sold for two pennies? Yet not one of them is forgotten by God. Indeed, the very hairs of your head are all numbered. Don't be afraid; you are worth more than many sparrows" (Luke 12:6-7).

She twisted strands of hair in her fingers.

"God made you the way he wanted you to be, and he loves you just as you are."

Society bombards our children with messages in various ways about good looks, body image, and what's considered attractive. But helping our children see themselves through eyes of divine love, as God's special creation, is intrinsic to helping them learn to accept themselves.

**Digging deeper:** Affirm your children in a special way today. Reflect with them on Psalm 139:13-18.

[ Gifts We Give Our Children ] **DAY** 171

# Jesus Understands

He was despised and rejected by mankind, a man
of suffering, and familiar with pain. (Isaiah 53:3)

"Why did she do that?" Nine-year-old Lisa burst out as we walked down a friend's driveway. "She could have called at least." Her voice trembled. I put my arm around her. Neither Jim nor I had any answers as she climbed into the van, her shoulders heaving.

We had found out that Lisa's friend from out-of-town had visited Atlanta and stayed with the family we had just visited. But she hadn't contacted us. Over the year since our relocation, though Lisa missed her friend, their correspondence had dwindled. We drove home to the sounds of sniffles and sobs.

When Lisa came downstairs for breakfast the next day, my heart sank when I saw her puffy, red eyes. *Lord, how can I help her?* I repeated my prayers from the previous night. *What can I say to ease the hurt?*

*I understand.* A soft whisper in my heart sparked hope. I reached across the kitchen table and put my hand over Lisa's.

"It must hurt a lot, but Jesus understands."

She stared at me with dull eyes.

"Remember how Judas, one of Jesus' disciples, betrayed him? And how three times Peter said he didn't know Jesus?"

I opened the Bible to Isaiah 53 and pointed out verse 3. "Even though Jesus died to give us life, we hurt him by the wrong things we do. Still he loves us and forgives us. 'Familiar with pain' means he knows what it's like to be hurt. People looked down on him and weren't kind to him."

Her fingers touched each word of the verse. When she lifted her head, her eyes were no longer dull. "I'm glad Jesus knows, Mama."

**Digging deeper:** What hope does the phrase "Jesus knows" offer you? Reflect on Luke 22:54-62.

[ Gifts We Give Our Children ] **DAY** 172

# Dealing with Hurt

The LORD is close to the brokenhearted. (Psalm 34:18)

Lisa's sadness over her friend not contacting her opened the door to a harsh reality of life—hurt. Though Jim and I ached for her, we knew we had to give her the tools to deal with life since it wouldn't be the last time she would be hurt. We took the following steps:

**We empathized.** Hurt is universal. According to 2 Corinthians 1:4, we can comfort "with the comfort we ourselves receive from God." Empathy shows our children that we love them and hurt for and with them, making them more open to our advice.

**We talked about it.** People deal with hurt in different ways. Some, like my daughter, need time before being willing to discuss it. Since Jim and I knew that love "always trusts, always hopes" (1 Corinthians 13:7), we encouraged Lisa to see the situation from another perspective. Our friends weren't obligated to tell us they were going to be in town—they had the freedom to do as they pleased; and perhaps they didn't have enough time to visit both families. They probably didn't mean to hurt Lisa by their lack of communication.

**We forgave.** We don't have control over others and their actions, but we can control our reactions. Hurt that isn't dealt with festers into bitterness (Hebrews 12:15). Ephesians 4:32 urges us to "Be kind and compassionate to one another, forgiving each other, just as in Christ God forgave you."

**We acted in love.** Often in emotional situations, it's hard for our actions to display forgiveness. But we are encouraged to live a life of love (Ephesians 5:2). God can heal our hurts and bind our wounds no matter how deep, because he is near the brokenhearted.

**Digging deeper:** How do you help your children deal with hurt? Reflect on Matthew 7:12.

# Through a Child's Eyes

"Truly I tell you, anyone who will not receive the kingdom
of God like a little child will never enter it." (Luke 18:17)

Our feet sank into the soggy carpet as we entered our living
room. Jim and I stared at each other as four-year-old Lisa
splashed her way through the house. "This is fun!" Her laughter
pealed through the house. "It's like having puddles inside!"

*How can she be so happy?* I thought as we surveyed the damage.

A torrential downpour had swept pine straw and mulch from
neighboring yards to ours. The debris formed a dam, backlog-
ging its progress downhill. The water had invaded our living
room and two bedrooms.

Late that night, I went into Lisa's bedroom, the hum of fans
and shop vacs in the background. She sat on the bed, her eyes
sparkling. "Mommy, what an adventure!"

"How can you say that?" Every bone in my body ached. I was
sick at the thought of replacing furniture and carpeting. "Do you
understand what happened?"

She nodded. "But Mama, I still have my room." I looked
around her room, crammed with furniture that we had salvaged
from the other rooms. In that split second, Jesus' words "Anyone
who will not receive the kingdom of God like a little child will
never enter it" took on new meaning.

After I kissed her and tucked her in, I shut the door behind me
and leaned against it. "She's right, Lord. It could have been
worse. We still have a roof over our heads. The kitchen and a
bedroom were spared. Friends helped. Please help me see life
through the eyes of a child."

**Digging deeper:** When has your child helped you get a better
perspective? Reflect on Habakkuk 3:17-18.

# A New Perspective

Be made new in the attitude of your minds. (Ephesians 4:23)

Though it has been years since our house was water-damaged, the incident and the lessons I learned from it are fresh in my mind.

**Choose to bless the Lord.** My daughter's view of the flood was different from mine, showing me that it's all a matter of perception. What a valuable lesson to remember when I'm frustrated with challenging school moments! That's when I need to stop and focus on the good. I'm blessed to homeschool: I'm with my children. I can shape their values. We have opportunities to talk anytime about whatever is on their minds, read, play, watch a movie, or just snuggle.

**"Rejoice in the Lord always,"** Paul encourages us several times in Philippians 3–4. The key to having a different perspective—whether it's over a soggy carpet or a not-so-good homeschooling day—is to find joy in the Lord. No matter what our circumstances may be, God is the one who gives joy and strength. The psalmist says, "You have filled my heart with greater joy than when their grain and new wine abound" (Psalm 4:8). Joy is not dependent on the situation; it's there despite it.

**Be renewed.** Paul urges us to put off our old way of life (Ephesians 4:22) and to be "made new in the attitude of [our] minds" (v. 23). I can choose to focus on the blessings and rejoice in the Lord only as my mind is renewed. It's a conscious, minute-to-minute putting on of "the new self, created to be like God in true righteousness and holiness" (v. 24).

**Digging deeper:** How does reflecting on Ephesians 4:22-24 help your perspective on challenging situations?

# Laughter's Power

A cheerful heart is good medicine, but a crushed
spirit dries up the bones. (Proverbs 17:22)

It was pizza and movie night. Peals of laughter and loud guffaws
echoed through our family room. At times we didn't know what
was more entertaining—the movie or our toddler who twirled
and shimmied to the music in the movie.

I turned to eleven-year-old Lisa, feeling her watching me.

"Mom, you're laughing uncontrollably," she giggled.

I held my sides as I nodded. We looked at each other and dis-
solved into laughter. Jim rolled his eyes, a grin teasing the corners
of his lips. Within minutes of the movie ending, he was on the
floor, wrestling with our toddler, Katy, whose squeals and giggles
filled the house. When he pretended to lie exhausted on the floor,
both girls attacked him. A jumble of limbs was all that was visible.

It was good to laugh together. The stress of trying to get things
done and get to activities on time fell away like unfettered chains.
The underlying tension as we weathered the ups and downs of
adolescence and school dissipated. We had connected as a family
again.

Laughter is like a breath of fresh air. It offers a fresh perspective on life and relaxes us. Laughing together can bring healing to
relationships. Proverbs likens a cheerful heart to "good medicine." Unlike most medications, it has no adverse side-effects. It
only brings good—a lighter heart and joy. Laughter is infectious.

**Digging deeper:** What does your family do for fun times?

# Courage

The LORD gave this command to Joshua son of Nun:
"Be strong and courageous, for you will bring the
Israelites into the land I promised them on oath,
and I myself will be with you." (Deuteronomy 31:23)

"Mommy." Eight-year-old Lisa stood in front of the bench, her
scooter by her side. As I scanned the perimeter of the park, I saw
her friends in the distance.

"What's wrong?" I reached for her.

"Nothing, Mommy. I just wanted to know if we could go to
the fountain on our scooters. You told me to stay close."

I smiled. "Thanks for coming back to check. As long as you're
with the other girls, you may go to the fountain."

She hopped on her scooter and was off.

When we drove home later, I asked her if the other girls
needed to get permission too.

"No, Mommy."

"How did you feel when you came to ask me?"

She looked out the window. "I felt stupid because they made
fun of me."

I reached out and patted her hand. "But you still came to ask
me. I'm proud of you. You did the right thing even though it was
hard."

Her smile lit up the van.

God commanded Joshua to "be strong and courageous" and
promised to be with him. The Hebrew phrase translated "be
strong and courageous" conveys the sense of being determined
and resolute.

Courage, I learned that day, wasn't the absence of fear; rather,
it was choosing to do what is right in spite of being afraid.

*Lord, give me the courage to follow you always.*

**Digging deeper:** How do your children display courage?

# Legacies

Let the one who is wise heed these things and
ponder the loving deeds of the LORD. (Psalm 107:43)

February 4, 2009. At twenty-nine degrees Fahrenheit, the biting
wind cut through every layer of clothing. Yet we joined others
walking toward Picnic Hill on Koinonia Farms in Southwest
Georgia. After almost a mile, we reached the summit, where an
unvarnished pine coffin lay adorned with a single long-stemmed
red rose and a hammer.

People of different races crowded around. Tears, laughter,
impromptu singing, and tributes warmed us as we gathered to
honor the life of one man whose obedience to God impacted millions all over the world.

Millard Fuller, a self-made millionaire at the age of twenty-
nine, gave away his fortune when his marriage encountered trou-
bled times. He moved with his family to Koinonia Farms, where
Clarence Jordan and *The Cotton Patch Gospel* influenced them.
Fuller later founded the nonprofit organization Habitat for
Humanity to show the love of Jesus in a tangible way.

Through his obedience, millions of people are blessed with a
"simple, decent house," a house with strong walls that can with-
stand the elements and a roof that doesn't leak or blow away or
through which snakes can fall.

Lives are changed—those who once had no hope gain dignity.
Children do better at school. Parents are motivated to pay off
their mortgages. People are introduced to Jesus, in whose name
the houses are built.

One man's obedience is still changing lives the world over.

What will your legacy be?

**Digging deeper:** Reflect on Psalm 102:18. Read *Building Materials
for Life* (volume 1) by Millard Fuller and *The Cotton Patch Gospel*
by Clarence Jordan.

# Your Reward

For what is our hope, our joy, or the crown in which we will glory
in the presence of our Lord Jesus when he comes? Is it not you?
Indeed, you are our glory and joy. (1 Thessalonians 2:19-20)

As Paul rejoiced in the Thessalonian believers, one day we too
will know such joy when we see the fruit of our homeschooling
labors.

May these words from homeschool graduates bless us:

"Homeschooling provides a strong foundation for life. It allows
parents to nurture their children in their faith. Through homeschooling, you have the flexibility to put the books down while
you focus on heart issues to develop good character."—Jonathan
Lewis, editor of *Homeschool Enrichment Magazine*

"The most important benefit is the privilege and responsibility of
godly parents who sacrifice to obey God's calling and daily pass on
their faith to their children. The process itself is the benefit. As we
talk of God and his Word, we are strengthened in our own faith.
The discipling relationship with our children challenges us to look
more to our heavenly Father for wisdom and grace.

"I am so grateful I am a homeschool graduate, but the greatest
blessing of all is being a homeschool mother."—Lea Ann Garfias,
homeschool mom of four

"Family, focus, and shelter are the benefits of homeschooling. Families can be together and build relationships in a way that few other
lifestyles allow. Children can focus on being kids, focus on following God, . . . and eventually focus on a particular academic bent or
preparation for a particular calling. I benefited from the latter.

"God intends parents, who are stronger and wiser, to shelter
their children and to walk alongside them into adulthood, teaching them to understand and cope with evil."—Rachel Starr Thomson, editor and author

**Digging deeper:** How does homeschooling benefit your family?

# God's Sure Presence

When Jacob awoke from his sleep, he thought, "Surely the LORD
is in this place, and I was not aware of it." (Genesis 28:16)

A month after we ended our first middle school year, the challenging moments bothered me. *Could school have been better? Could I
have approached the problems with more grace?* Guilt replaced the joy
of finishing another year and experiencing God's faithfulness.

Weeks later, Jacob's words in Genesis 28:16 resonated with me
long after my devotions ended. Images from our school year
flickered in the back of my mind, but this time with a difference.

Those difficult moments as we grappled with math were step-
pingstones to rely on God's strength and to experience the power
of prayer.

The months with iritis were blessings in disguise. Though having dilated eyes 24/7 had slowed school and my writing, stepping back helped me reevaluate and reprioritize. The possibility
of losing my sight drew me closer to the Lord.

The challenging moments of adolescence were opportunities for
us to search our hearts and seek more of God's grace in our lives.

The times I wondered if I was getting through to Lisa were
occasions to allow God to grip her heart with his love.

I may not have had as dramatic an encounter as Jacob, but the
presence of the Lord was surely with us through the ups and
downs of school. I hadn't seen it until now. The Lord's promise to
Jacob was mine, too, for every step of my homeschooling journey.
"I am with you and will watch over you wherever you go. . . . I
will not leave you until I have done what I have promised you"
(Genesis 28:15).

**Digging deeper:** When were you unaware of God's sure presence?
Reflect on Genesis 28:10-22.

# Ebenezer

Then Samuel took a stone and set it up between
Mizpah and Shen. He named it Ebenezer, saying,
"Thus far the LORD has helped us." (1 Samuel 7:12)

*Seven years and still counting!* As I marked off our one hundred
eightieth school day at the end of sixth grade, my mind traveled
back to the first day Lisa and I had walked toward our schoolroom
hand in hand. Never could I have imagined then that our homeschooling journey would continue into middle school. I bowed my
head and whispered, "Lord, thank you for bringing us this far."

In the Old Testament, the Israelites constructed memorials to
remind them of God's faithfulness. In 1 Samuel 7, Samuel set up
a stone—"Ebenezer" or "stone of help"—to commemorate an
amazing victory. "The LORD thundered with loud thunder
against the Philistines and threw them into such a panic that they
were routed before the Israelites" (1 Samuel 7:10).

So, at the end of each school year, Lisa and I take a few minutes to consider God's faithfulness:

"God gave us our co-op and friends."
"God gave me a baby sister."
"The Lord helped the middle school co-op kids get enough
toys for the Christmas toy drive."
"God kept us safe in India."
"Jesus helped me in math."

The answers change over the years, but these Ebenezers never
fail to encourage us. They are testimony that during the times I
am overwhelmed, Jesus leads me to the Rock that is higher than
I. Because "it is God who arms me with strength and makes my
way perfect" (Psalm 18:32), no matter what our homeschool days
may be like, I can say at the end of the year, "Praise be to my
Rock! Exalted be God, the Rock, my Savior!" (2 Samuel 22:47).

**Digging deeper:** What are some of your Ebenezers?

# Index

## Homeschool and You

## Homeschool Foundations

Day 2
Day 14
Day 21
Day 22
Day 29
Day 56
Day 57
Day 68
Day 69
Day 76
Day 131
Day 132
Day 133
Day 134
Day 135
Day 139
Day 144
Day 167

## Homeschool and Family

Day 3
Day 9
Day 15
Day 26
Day 35
Day 43
Day 49
Day 88
Day 105
Day 113
Day 120
Day 127
Day 137
Day 148
Day 149
Day 175

## Gifts We Give Our Children

Day 4
Day 10
Day 28
Day 40
Day 58
Day 73
Day 81
Day 83
Day 85
Day 97
Day 98
Day 99
Day 111
Day 115
Day 116
Day 117
Day 136
Day 140
Day 147
Day 152
Day 155
Day 161
Day 162
Day 168
Day 169
Day 170
Day 171
Day 172
Day 177

| Spiritual Vitamins | Homeschool Basics |
|:---:|:---:|
| Day 5 | Day 6 |
| Day 45 | Day 7 |
| Day 55 | Day 11 |
| Day 70 | Day 12 |
| Day 75 | Day 16 |
| Day 80 | Day 17 |
| Day 82 | Day 18 |
| Day 84 | Day 20 |
| Day 95 | Day 33 |
| Day 110 | Day 34 |
| Day 114 | Day 38 |
| Day 121 | Day 39 |
| Day 123 | Day 41 |
| Day 124 | Day 42 |
| Day 125 | Day 46 |
| Day 130 | Day 61 |
| Day 138 | Day 62 |
| Day 159 | Day 63 |
| Day 174 | Day 64 |
|  | Day 65 |
|  | Day 77 |
|  | Day 78 |
|  | Day 86 |
|  | Day 92 |
|  | Day 93 |
|  | Day 94 |
|  | Day 101 |
|  | Day 102 |
|  | Day 112 |
|  | Day 142 |
|  | Day 163 |
|  | Day 166 |

## And a Child Will Lead Them

Day 50
Day 79
Day 145
Day 151
Day 154
Day 173
Day 176

## A Faith of Their Own

Day 51
Day 52
Day 53
Day 54
Day 59
Day 72
Day 74
Day 118
Day 122